T0194287

HEDGE
About
SATAN

LINCOLN SMITH

WESTBOW
PRESS®
A DIVISION OF THOMAS NELSON
& ZONDERVAN

WestBow Press books may be ordered through booksellers or by contacting:

WestBow Press
A Division of Thomas Nelson & Zondervan
1663 Liberty Drive
Bloomington, IN 47403
www.westbowpress.com
1 (866) 928-1240

Scripture taken from the King James Version of the Bible.

ISBN: 978-1-9736-5119-2 (sc)
ISBN: 978-1-9736-5120-8 (hc)
ISBN: 978-1-9736-5118-5 (e)

Library of Congress Control Number: 2019900438

Print information available on the last page.

WestBow Press rev. date: 2/15/2019

To my loving family who always provide such great support, and my friend in Christ, Patrick, who helped to start this book with various revisions and suggestions, I thank you all.

CONTENTS

CHAPTER 1

EASY BELIEVISM

The core message of this book is aimed against Satan while also serving as a call for God's true church to move away from spiritual complacency. Never in the history of the church has there been such meddling and darkening of God's counsel. Outside the church, Satan holds sway in binding people to earth with the endless cares and trials of this life which is devoid of even a thought or contemplation for our Creator, "in whom the god of this world hath blinded the minds of them which believe not, lest the light of the glorious gospel of Christ, who is the image of God, should shine unto them" (2 Corinthians 4:4).

Countless examples, such as secular humanism, false religions, atheism, scientific reasoning and any other form of darkness all combine to squash down, fade out and marginalize His Word. Through such deception, Satan places man as the central and pinnacle focus above God, is something that he has proactively built upon since the fall and will remain here on earth until the final judgment. That is when all anti-God forces and those held under its evil sway, will be torn down in righteous indignation, "And the angels which kept not their first estate, but left their own habitation, he hath reserved in everlasting chains under darkness unto the judgment of the great day" (Jude verse: 6).

Our concern, however, must be for God's true church here on earth for never before has the church been so marginalized and derided in bearing an influence across society. In several Asian regions, including China, parts of Africa, and India, the church is vibrantly growing amidst persecution, but in the west, it appears the church has been overshadowed to a time reminiscent of the dark ages when the Roman Catholic church withheld God's Word from society.

A great reformation of the church occurred after this period where many Godly men came to the fore to attack the darkness and move the church back into a greater and deeper doctrinal alignment to His Word. Martin Luther, John Calvin, and William Tyndale were great reformers from this time, but only by the Grace of God that worked in them. God's Word also became more freely available throughout society.

Moving forward to today, Australia, like many other countries, has now legalized same sex marriage, to which our Parliament in 2017 joined in unison of song, "We are one, but we are many…" – (We are Australian). Yet where is our voice of passion and Christian triumph? Do we really sing praise to the King of glory who is the "Alpha and Omega" (Revelation 1:11) over universal and worldwide governance and directive? And the reason for such impotence is Satan having successfully compromised Scripture to cater for the standards of the world instead of Scripture being kept separate and used as a reproof against such ungodly practice, "All scripture is given by inspiration of God, and is profitable for doctrine, for reproof, for correction, for instruction in righteousness" (2 Timothy 3:16).

COMPROMISE: -

The church itself must also bear a large portion of responsibility for such compromise and immersion with the world. For example, in catering for the flesh, worldly entertainment arises where the distinction between the saved and unsaved in membership is ignored. This leaves the saved as an alienated minority that is eventually forced to leave the church that now holds to a very shallow standing in the Word in succumbing to worldliness over spiritual needs. In seeking cultural relevance and acceptance, many New Calvinist pastors and church leaders within large contemporary, or megachurches, have sadly left off God's authoritative Word as the regulative and true foundation of worship in favor of both worldly pursuits and thinking.

Satan knows man's love for numbers for which one former contemporary worship leader calls both "unproductive and divisive." [1] Unproductive is an interesting analogy, for despite such large numbers one may rightly ask, is there really a true saving faith, or reverence, attached to such activity?

Charismatic churches hold to fresh visions, revelations, and healings that sit alongside and weaken the Gospel. Yet, in most contemporary or megachurches, it is both a hypocritical and sentimental love, through a religious synchronism and assimilation with the world, that derides the Gospel. True and discerning love rejoices solely in His Word and stands sure and stable in the doctrines of Grace that set believers apart in salvation. "Divine worship must be such as God himself has appointed, else it is offering strange fire. Lev 10:1: He must not leave out anything in the pattern, nor add to it...If God was so exact and curious about the place of worship, how exact will he be about the matter of his worship! Surely here everything must be according to the pattern prescribed in his word." [2]

As represented by Cain's vengeance and anger in slaying Abel in Genesis 4, the seed of the serpent has always persecuted the seed of the women to impede its spread. Although he is prevented and restrained by God's faithfulness and sovereign will from doing so (more fully discussed in chapter 2), and his final doom

---

[1] Dan Lucarni, *Why I left the Contemporary Christian Music Movement*, Evangelical Press, 2002, p. 19.

[2] Thomas Watson, *Body of Divinity*, Christian Classics Ethereal Library, https://www.ccel.org/ccel/watson/divinity.html, first published 1686, p. 14.

is clearly prophesied throughout Scripture, Satan still maintains his ultimate aim and desire to darken and expunge God's Word and it's validity by any means and force available. The destructive influence of New Calvinism is one such weapon that certainly pervades many contemporary churches, whereby, a denial of our Lord's penal substitution, along with His eternal Sonship, adds doctrinal heresy into their broad mix of error.

So this book is a call to arms, in the spiritual context of course. "Move Back Satan, and rise up church!" must be our call. What shall stand, a false and Satanically led and infiltrated church movement with instability and compromise to worldly standards, or Christ's uncompromising, visible and militant true church movement standing firm in His Word to conquer hearts and, thereby, fulfill His faithful and sovereign will in salvation?

Where do our priorities really lie? for reaffirmation of God's Word, not assimilation, is key. Biblical separation determines a walk of faith that is not entangled with, and stands in complete contrast to, the fashions and trends of worldliness. "The professing church has lost the respect of sinners because far too many Christians have lost sight of their calling and have been pressed into the mould of things about them. We need to be reminded that the church is a called out organism…And if the church has been called from something, it has also been called to something, i.e., to holy living that God may be glorified in her actions." [3]

Believers must keep an overall and eternal perspective on events and circumstance as souls are being lost to everlasting damnation on a disproportionate scale, compared to the evangelistic reasoning and fervor (or lack thereof) displayed by the church militant. Consider the spread of Islam for example. A simple Internet search suggests nearly two billion souls are converted worldwide and adhering to its dark counsels, all lost

[3] William E Cox, *Amillennialism Today*, Presbyterian and Reformed Publishing Co., 1966,.pp. 53-54.

and heading in the wrong direction in the name of false religion. Our Lord's great commission is a duty and calling for His people to reach out to the lost, "Go ye into all the world, and preach the gospel to every creature" (Mark 16:15).

Yet has the general state of easy believism blinded this call of soul winning through unstable and impotent evangelism, a position where Satan would have us be? Having God on your own terms is the attitude that essentially pervades many churches through ecumenicalism, the prosperity Gospel, and various seeker sensitive outlooks. An example of the subtlety by which error is introduced is the joint ecumenical manifesto known as the Manhattan Declaration that was ratified by many prominent Orthodox, Catholic and Evangelical signatories in 2009. In presenting such a unified front on common beliefs against abortion and same-sex marriage, however, discernment is lost and apostasy is drawn when fundamental theological differences concerning the Gospel are overshadowed.

Many contemporary church leaders also propagate Christian teaching that extends the great commission "to include the unauthorised task of global social restoration." [4] Such a spirit of the age in calling for social justice is not in line with the true and vital work of the Spirit which applies Grace upon the soul in salvation and progressive sanctification that yields itself to the righteous and moral commands of Christ in bearing His likeness and image through the fruits of true holiness: –

> "But we all, with open face beholding as in a glass
> the glory of the Lord, are changed into the same
> image from glory to glory, even as by the Spirit of
> the Lord" (2 Corinthians 3:18).

---

[4] E. S Williams *The New Calvinists, Changing the Gospel,* Wakeman Trust & Belmont House, 2014, p. 28.

SIN: -

Fundamentally, punishment for sin is in perfect accord with God's authority and justice which is binding upon humans by the rule of law, or the covenant of works. This has two aspects. Firstly, it comprises the Tree of the Knowledge of Good and Evil where Adam's transgression and violation of God's command not to eat from the Tree, did bear original sin into the world and, thereby, impute the consequence of death to man.

Secondly, it comprises of the moral law as given to Moses in the Ten Commandments on Mount Sinai. God's known will, as revealed through the universal precepts of the law, represent the duty of man and are founded upon the absolute nature of God's justice as an expression of His perfect, holy and righteous character. As nobody can uphold such moral obligation and ordinance, Christ, in satisfying such righteous commands by His propitiatory death, has removed the threat of everlasting death as the penalty of transgression from the law for His blood brought people.

The Gospel, therefore, replaces Adam as our fallen and natural head to that of Christ who in full obedience fulfills all mandates of the law in righteousness, that He both demands and provides, by offering Himself as a sacrifice for sin. He is our true covenant head for just as death was imputed to the posterity of Adam after the natural seed after the fall, so does Christ's vicarious death lead captivity captive by imputing righteousness to His spiritual seed as those who believe on Him by faith. "As the law demands righteousness, to impute or ascribe righteousness to anyone, is, in scriptural language, to justify," [5] whereby, Christ also enlightens the conscience away from dead works in the forgiveness of all of our sins which brings forth peace and assurance: -

---

[5] Charles Hodge, *Justification, the Law and the Righteousness of Christ*, http://www.chapellibrary.org/book/jtla, 1998, p. 2.

> "And you, being dead in your sins and the uncircumcision of your flesh, hath he quickened together with him, having forgiven you all trespasses" (Colossians 2:13).

Such Grace perfectly manifests God's love towards unworthy sinners as the sentence of life is pronounced upon a believer who now stands eternally justified and accepted before Him.

Righteousness and justification are, therefore, one and the same for Christ's blood sake: –

> "I am crucified with Christ: nevertheless, I live; yet not I, but Christ liveth in me: and the life which I now live in the flesh I live by the faith of the Son of God, who loved me, and gave himself for me" (Galatians 2:20).

The Kingdom of heaven is apprehended by faith by which believers are obliged to uphold, as a rule of life, all manner of righteous duty that mirrors a likeness to Christ and His righteousness that is imputed at conversion: –

> "And that he died for all, that they which live should not henceforth live unto themselves, but unto him which died for them, and rose again" (2 Corinthians 5:15).

Although real and acceptable obedience is not possible before conversion due to our sin and moral corruption before God, the implication of the law as fulfilled by Christ is significant for it determines an ultimate test, or settled attitude, by which a believer may be judged as to their standing or falling in relation to the Kingdom of God. It is certainly not an entry into the Kingdom, for the remission of sin is solely dependent upon Christ's atonement and His shed blood, but this measure of our spiritual attitude and reverence answers to what God has written upon our heart towards obedience.

Despite the experience of true conversion, many believers today remain stagnant and do not grow in Grace and in the understanding of the doctrines of salvation upon which our faith does lie. Such instability not only means that many believers are easily carried away with the fashions, and trends of the world, but it also fails the Spirit truly applying sanctifying Grace upon the heart as our chief delight when believers earnestly seek to be like Him in consecrating a wholly and separate distinctiveness from the world, "I am the vine, ye are the branches: He that abideth in me, and I in him, the same bringeth forth much fruit: for without me ye can do nothing" (John 15:5). It is such a joyful expression of filial love for God to see his children truly walk in sanctifying Grace.

MODERNISM: -

On a corporate level, prayer must resonate from our churches where many, and not just a few, attend regular prayer meetings, but also where many zealously participate with a desire for true obedience to His will in saving souls. Jacob like wrestling in prayer "until the breaking of day" (Genesis 32:24) is so lacking for the blessing of true spiritual obedience to stand firm against the sway and bear true light in this fallen world. Jacob thought little as to any question whether it was in the power of God to fulfill his petition(s), yet such a question and doubt must arise when the power and authority of God's Word is diminished from a materialistic standing that underlies many contemporary churches. Another dramatic influence of Satan on the church is modernism that has given rise to theological liberalism (more fully discussed in chapter 3), but the essential cause is where "liberal minded churchgoers argued that the Christian religion needed to adapt to modern ideas in to survive." [6]

Contextualization of the Bible has also arisen from particular church organizations like the World Council of churches that was founded in 1948 with the strongly ecumenical aim of unifying churches across the globe. From the various assemblies that followed, both key doctrine and the overall purpose of Scripture were watered down to suit both social and humanistic means. Adopting and modifying Gospel presentation according to such New Evangelical cultural sensitivity and political correctness blunts the effectual and spiritual power of the Gospel to transform lives.

The following definition of salvation that was given at the Bangkok Assembly over the new year of 1972-73 highlights how such an inoffensive Gospel is thus propagated where forgiveness for sin is not referred: - "Section II depicts salvation in 4 dimensions. It manifests itself in the struggle for (1) economic justice against exploitation; (2) for human dignity against oppression; (3) for solidarity against alienation; and (4) for hope against despair in personal life (WCC 1973:19). In the process of salvation, we must relate (only?) these four dimensions to each other." [7]

A further undermining of God's Word comes from proponents of antinomianism who say that as a Christian is under Grace, he is at liberty and no is longer under God's moral law as expressed in the Ten Commandments. Reformed theology suggests, however, that such a breach and reneging of moral obligation is not Gospel centered and will only weaken sanctification by drawing believers back into fellowship with the world, for which the Apostle John warns, "Love not the world, neither the things that are in the world" (1 John 2:15).

---

[6] E. S Williams, *Holistic Mission, Weighed in the Balances*, Belmont House Publishing, 2016, p. 35.

[7] E. S Williams, *Holistic Mission*, ibid., p. 133.

Our attitude to Him mirrors that of our attitude to His law so prioritizing time for prayer and the reading of God's Word, as opposed to unproductive time on the Internet and social media sites etc., are simple yet fundamental steps in overcoming the world. The altar to our heart must resonate with Christ or else Satan will tamper and deride our joy: –

> "Whom having not seen, ye love; in whom, though now ye see him not, yet believing, ye rejoice with joy unspeakable and full of glory" (1 Peter 1:8).

It is a perfectly natural thought to inquire more of salvation and it is certainly no great sleight or force field to cross, to come unto Him you who "are heavy laden" and He "will give you rest" (Matthew 11:28). The world cannot possibly know true peace like this, and as our Lord says, "They are not of the world, even as I am not of the world" (John 17:16) (the stages of conversion are discussed in chapter 4).

The believers' great battle within and against our flesh nature, along with Satan's desire to draw moral transgression and lapse, begins immediately after conversion, but in contending with the activities of Satan, I should like to follow the example of Michael the archangel, who "durst not bring against him a railing accusation, but said, the Lord rebuke thee" (Jude verse: 9). God's unknown will, or the will of God's decree, was eternally foreordained from before the foundations of the world: -

> "I was set up from everlasting, from the beginning, or ever the earth was" (Proverbs 8:23).

His decree is both immutable and effectual in that everything included in it will certainly come to pass and it is also hidden in God as only He does know who will receive His eternal mercy in salvation, for "Known unto God are all works from the beginning of the world" (Acts 15:18). "He chose the ones he did simply because He chose to choose them." [8]

God's everlasting decree is twofold in nature that stems from His unfailing promise of mercy. First, the covenant of redemption, or the blessed counsel of peace, is an eternal agreement between God the Father and the Son (more fully discussed in chapter 5).

Secondly, the covenant of Grace as God's agreement with the elect, and, thereby, mankind, is enacted through the conditions by which are met through what Christ has fulfilled in His agreement with God the Father.

Belief and "all the inward excellence of the Christian, along with the fruits of the Spirit, are the consequences—and not the causes—of his reconciliation and acceptance with God. They are the robe of beauty, the white garment, with which Christ arrays those who come to Him poor, and blind, and naked." [9] The work of the Holy Spirit is also needed "to bring the sinner to Christ, to overcome his innate opposition and to accept the provision God has made." [10]

Such ordination and foreknowledge determine our election as both eternally and effectually secure, "The preparations of the heart in man, and the answer of the tongue, is from the Lord" (Proverbs 16:1) and as nothing can thwart His sovereign purpose, Satan is left as a fallen and defeated foe. Our Savior's sinless obedience and sacrificial death restores life, whereby, the terrible consequence of Satan's yoke and dominion over death, is annihilated for the host of His elect who, as previous captives, are eternally released by His sovereign mercy: -

---

[8] A. W. Pink, *The Sovereignty of God,* Banner of Truth Trust, Reprinted 1998, p. 55.

[9] Charles. Hodge, ibid., p. 4.

[10] A. W. Pink, ibid., pp. 72-73.

"that through death he might destroy him that had the power of death, that is the devil" (Hebrews 2:14).

Despite this incredible and condescending mercy and love of Christ, however, the force of Satan's restrained influence or probation still holds significant consequence in this present Gospel age before our Lord's return, for there will be a period of great tribulation and deception, "which but for the elect's sake shall be shortened" (Matthew 24:22). Our Lord further confirms this great period of apostasy and falling away by asking, "Nevertheless, when the Son of man cometh, shall he find faith on the earth?" (Luke 18:8). This suggests that there will be a tiny exercise of faith by believers at the time of His return, who may hold even more liberal and rational beliefs than today as a result of such open-minded and modern opinions that deride the authority of God's Word and the extent of anti-Christian legislation as inveighed by Satan.

Such a warning for complacency is given against the church of Laodicea, who "art lukewarm, and neither cold nor hot, I will spue thee out of my mouth" (Revelation 3:16). "A lukewarm professor is one that serves God and mammon; that halts between two opinions, and knows not what religion is best, and cares little for any, yet keeps in a round of duty, though indifferent to it, and contents himself with it." [11] It is not a profession but fruitfulness that brings glory to God and is why such immersion with worldliness, along with a liberal application to His Word, is a great blight on the church today, as a failure to bear true salt and light is a mirror to the steep moral decline we see across society today.

Does the reproof of the church of Laodicea represent the last phase of the church age, for although there were many true

---

[11] John Gill, Exposition of the Bible Commentary, https://www. biblestudytools.com/commentaries/gills-exposition-of-the-bible/Revelation 3.16 (accessed September 14, 2018).

believers at Laodicea, and it was not stone cold or heretical as the Gospel was preached, it was caught in between, in a state of flux as "neither cold nor hot" by not being truly loyal and separate in holiness. Such apostasy, self-confidence, and compromise is certainly in line with the impotent and destitute state of the church in recent times concerning true soul winning and evangelism and will rightly burn as stubble against His fiery indignation in judgment, "as wretched, and miserable, and poor, and blind, and naked" (Revelation 3:17).

Nobody does know His return except that it will be in the twinkling of an eye, yet as a symbol of completeness, the church of Laodicea is also the seventh and final church mentioned, so we must fervently use what time is left to proclaim His Gospel far and wide so the many more souls are converted and sanctified until "the fullness of the Gentiles be come in" (Romans 11:25).

This verse can also apply to primarily western churches who must take heed of the warning given to Israel, who through their self-righteous and proud religious leaders spurned their many privileges through blindness and conceit, "which in part is happened to Israel" (Romans 11:25). Their overzealous and meticulous observance to the ancient sacrificial law and temple order neglected true repentance upon the heart and is an example given to the Gentiles themselves against such similar apostasy and false religious activity.

This blindness that happened to ethnic Israel befell them not by chance either, but by the will of God's everlasting decree, "whom he will hardeneth" (Romans 9:18). Notwithstanding, God's faithfully in preserves a "remnant according to the election of grace" (Romans 11:5) as seen through the typical church, or true Israel, that did resonate from the Jewish age of the church (more fully discussed in chapter 6). In turning from sin, the remnant saw Grace throughout the various types and shadows of the Old Testament law.

Today there are so many denials of true faith and doctrine

that believers can be led aside into compromise by all manner of false doctrine and heretical teaching, "For there shall arise false Christ's and false prophets and shall shew great signs and wonders; insomuch if it were possible, they shall deceive the very elect" (Matthew 24:24). But considering the great gifts and blessings of sanctifying Grace bestowed upon the bride of His elect by the Spirit, along with the security and preservation of His Almighty and sustaining hand, our final and total deception is impossible for we are eternally preserved and sanctified by a decree in righteousness that cannot diminish: –

> "Let my beloved come into his garden, and eat his pleasant fruits" (Song of Solomon 4:16).

Satan and worldliness within the church will only be hedged about if we stand in prayerful dependence upon Him and prove obedience to His eternal call which is by Grace alone, through Faith alone, in Christ alone!

CHAPTER 2

LUCIFER TURNED SATAN

Scripture draws a monumental line of separation between God's true church here on earth and the synagogue of Satan. This judgment is pronounced upon Satan early in Scripture through Grace, "I shall put enmity between thee and the women, and between thy seed and her seed" (Genesis 3:15). That such separation exists between the two seeds is evident, and much suffering is foretold by the enmity excited thereby, for God's realm of light and truth stands opposed to, and is often drawn into conflict with, the ungodly realm of darkness and evil. It is, however, through such opposition and persecution, that God's true church shines like a burning and eternal light that Christ has determined and desires it to be.

God was not obligated to permit the fall for evil and darkness to enter this world to show forth His glorious power and unchanging, mercy and love. It was His sovereign purpose which made it so for He allows and permits Satan's restrained activity to bring persecution upon the church. We must begin to understand God's perspective, for, without such conflict, no glorious and everlasting light could possibly shine or reverberate around the world, and it is a very important aspect of His absolute and sovereign purpose to bring glory to Himself amidst such darkness: –

"For God, who commanded the light to shine out of darkness hath shined in our hearts, to give the light of the glory of God in the face of Jesus Christ" (2 Corinthians 4:6).

"He must bring the light of heaven into contact with darkness; so as to necessitate a trial of strength between the powers of evil working in them, and the truth and Grace of God as displayed in Christ." [12]

A God who is limited, or who limits Himself is not the God of the Bible, nor is He sovereign: –

"I form the light, and create darkness, I make peace and create evil: I the Lord do all these things" (Isaiah 45:7).

God's decree is immutable and nothing, therefore, is outside of His control for He has salvation and damnation in His power: -

"But God is the judge: he putteth down one and setteth up another" (Psalm 75:7).

God's power is also inexhaustible; it is never spent or wasted: -

"Trust ye in the Lord forever: for in the Lord JE-HO-VAH is everlasting strength" (Isaiah 26:4).

The Devil cannot circumvent nor overcome any of God's

---

[12] Patrick Fairbairn, *The Visions of Ezekiel*, Wakeman Great Reprints, first published 1851, p. 427.

sovereign decree, which follows through to his judgment, and as his time of assault and antagonism towards God's true church is limited, the following 6 passages help to determine the exact nature of our great enemy and adversary: -

1. Preceding his fall, he was "in Eden the garden of God." He was "the anointed cherub that covereth; and I have set thee so: so thou was upon the holy mountain of God" ..."Thou wast perfect in thy ways from the day that thou wast created, till iniquity was found in thee"..."Thine heart is lifted up because of thy beauty, thou hast corrupted thy wisdom by reason of thy brightness" (Ezekiel 28:13-17).

2. "How you have fallen from heaven, O Lucifer, son of the morning! How art thou cut down to the ground, which did weaken the nations! For thou hast said in thine heart, I will exalt my throne above the stars of God: I will also sit upon the mount of the congregation... I will ascend above the heights of the clouds; I will be like the most High" (Isaiah 14:12-14).

3. Our Lord further describes his fall, "The seventy returned with joy saying, Lord even the devils are subject to us through thy name. And he said to them, I was watching Satan as lightning fall from heaven" (Luke 10:17-18).

Lucifer, who at this point is named "son of the morning," was given some authority by the Lord as an "anointed" or "covering" cherub (Ezekiel 28:14). We can ascertain that his fall from heaven was a reneging of this authority from God in preference to creating his own dominion, for he holds visions of grandeur of wanting to "exalt" his "throne above the stars of God" (Isaiah 14:13). Lucifer, in becoming impressed with his own beauty, wanted the honor and glory that belongs to God alone and his fall represents his great corruption of self-generated pride and disobedience,

"Because thine heart is lifted up, and thou hast said, I am a God, I sit in the seat of God, in the midst of the seas" (Ezekiel 28:2).

Angels are created beings, "Thus the heavens and the earth were finished, and all the host of them" (Genesis 2:1) and as a consequence of his heinous sin, Lucifer's name is now changed to Satan (meaning adversary). His self-will against God is the point where sin actually enters the universe and this first act of apostasy draws the darkness and spirit of anti-Christ that is to follow. Satan's banishment from heaven precedes the fall of man by an indeterminate period of time, before, in the form of a serpent, he does tempt Eve, and, thereby, God's earthly image Adam, into sin and corruption in the garden of Eden.

Man's part in the fall cannot be overlooked either as the covenant of works, or covenant obedience, to obey God's command relating to the rule of the knowledge of good and evil, as implanted in Adam through the inward law, would soon have been broken regardless of Satan's action in beguiling Eve. God tested the loyalty obedience of Adam in order for him to sustain his blessed and eternal life in righteousness, for as His creation, the creature is to be fully satisfied with God's provision, and not reflect on our own wants or desires.

That both an external and internal obedience was required by the tendency of such a divine precept is seen in three ways: –

Firstly, every single part of man is to uphold this command; Secondly, it is to be upheld in the highest degree of our action and nature. Thirdly, with full perseverance in true love to God; "Man's trite happiness is to be placed in God alone and nothing is to be desired aside from submission to God and in order to employ it for Him." [13] Man must be satisfied even without the most delightful and desirable things if God so commands, "For

---

[13] A. W Pink, *The Doctrine of Human Depravity*, Chapel Library, http://www.chapellibrary.org/book/dohd, 1998, p. 8.

the work of a man shall render unto him, and cause every man to find according to his ways" (Job 34:11).

Adam was created as a rational and never dying soul with perfect wisdom, holiness, righteous knowledge of God and he had dominion over the animals as commissioned by God. "In unfallen Adam, the will was free, free in both directions, free toward good and free towards evil." [14] He was king of this garden paradise who had complete power and freedom to retain his integrity, which he traded in his pre-fallen state for that of self-love and self-exaltation. In a single act of rebellion and disobedience, both Adam and Eve turned away from the Tree of Life and lost the image of God from creation. As our representative head, punishment for Adam's sin is in perfect accord with God's authority and justice for the immediate penal sanction administered not only imputes corporeal death to the body but also spiritual death to the soul of all mankind.

The kingdom he once ruled and held dominion over now rebels against Adam as he is cast forth from the garden, and although an entail of woe is placed upon the posterity of man through such wicked defection and apostasy, there is still an offer of mercy from death through redemptive Grace. There is no such offer of mercy for Satan, however, who, despite taking over dominion over the earth, now faces certain judgment as pronounced in Genesis 3:15. From Satan's tirade with man, along with his adversity and resistance to God, have arisen many anti-values and anti-standards from sins such as lust, pride, disobedience, fornication, covetousness, murder, and self-will, all of which did emanate through the fall.

Satan will take any opportunity to encroach man up in his own vanity and conceit, for which man will forever fall over himself to follow, "because iniquity shall abound, the love of many shall wax cold" (Matthew 24:12). Satan has been observing man for many

---

[14] A. W. Pink, *The Sovereignty of God,* ibid., p. 99.

centuries and it is the same base tricks and alluring baits that are applied over and over again for man's fallen and corrupt nature is the same and the flesh is deftly betrayed. Like a moth to the flame is a good analogy for we all, so weakly, consent to his destructive will with all our hearts and minds.

Man, however, must further contend with the significant person of Satan, who is not alone as the following passages indicate: -

4. "And his tail drew the third part of heaven, and did cast them to the earth: and the dragon did stand before the women which was ready to be delivered, for to devour her child as soon as she was born" (Revelation 12:4).

5. "And there was war in heaven: Michael and his angels fought against the dragon; and the dragon fought and his angels, and prevailed not; neither was their place found any more in heaven. And the great dragon was cast out, that old serpent, called the Devil, and Satan, which deceiveth the whole world: he was cast out into the earth, and his angels were cast out with him" (Revelation 12:7-9).

Angels are all "ministering spirits" (Hebrews 1:14) around God's throne to bring Him glory. They are God's servants, His messengers, and His chariot to perform His will. Satan, who does not have the power or capacity to become incarnate in the flesh, also has representatives to bid his control on earth through multiple minions, demons or nominees that make him so powerful a force of darkness for after his encounter with Michael, he took one third of the angels with him at his fall, a number that cannot be quantified. "For if God spared not the angels that sinned, but cast them down to hell, and delivered them into chains of darkness, to be reserved unto judgment" (2 Peter 2:4). "They are called, 'morning stars' (Job 38:8) but 'falling stars;' they were holy, but mutable. As the vessel is overturned with the sail, so their sails being swelled with pride, they were overturned." [15]

Satan's willing agents are bidding his wicked cause in countless positions and vantage points and added to this is the ease in which the creature is blindly led astray to vainglory like a lost sheep. Satan is indefatigably earnest in his quest for darkness, he is never half-hearted and he never wastes a day. Above all else, the earth is his domain where he has helped programme man to think primarily of earthly comfort and physical wellbeing.

Western society is so innately bound and so self-absorbed within itself that it represents a 'generation me' mindset and culture that is squarely attuned for the here and now. It is desperately devoid of any serious eternal consideration and consequence ahead, whereby, any true Christian testimony will always radiate much light amidst such bleak and ruinous surrounds. Man may be anarchic by nature yet God through our inner constitution has mercifully written a general principle of law and order by which society is generally restrained from absolute corruption and anarchy by an innate willingness to be governed by laws.

MAN'S RESTRAINT: -

Through the law of nature as written upon the heart there exists a certain level of morality that can decipher between good and evil and also maintains some compassion and concern for law and order through such commands like, "Thou shalt not kill;" "Thou shalt not commit adultery;" "Thou shalt not steal" etc., "For when the Gentiles, which have not the law, do by nature the things contained in the law, these, having not the law, are a law unto themselves" (Romans 2:14).

Nobody can uphold such morality and demands of the law to its entirety for the natural inclination of man does pick and choose

---

[15] Thomas Watson, ibid., p. 10.

such standards whilst also deciding which ones they will follow, and reject, at their (subjective) will: –

> "Why do the heathen rage, and the people imagine
> a vain thing?" (Psalm 2:1).

God is, therefore, perfectly justified in His condemnation of such corrosion, for the conscience itself bears witness to the dictates of God's law as etched upon the heart, "their thoughts the mean while accusing or else excusing one another" (Romans 2:15). "The conscience is a favourable witness concerning good deeds, for in that case their thoughts either excuse or defend them. It a condemning witness when they do evil works for their thoughts accuse them, and their conscience torments them." [16]

Over time, however, natural man's conscience becomes deadened and seared by sin, whereby, our gracious Creator and the supreme being, out of necessity, voluntarily condescends to guide and accommodate the creature in what he should do in order to imitate and follow Him. Otherwise, man would end up as self-autonomous and lawless in doing and making decisions as he likes: -

> "Who would not fear thee, O King of the nations?
> For to thee doth it appertain: forasmuch as among
> all the wise men of the nations, and in all their
> kingdoms, there is none like unto thee" (Jeremiah
> 10:7).

Such a distinction is drawn between the Creator's perfect, holy, and righteous character through both the holy law as inscribed upon the heart and the Mosaic law that express His nature and absolute justice against the sin of His creation. Natural man,

---

[16] Martin Luther, *Commentary on Romans*, Kregel Classics, 1954, p. 60.

therefore, stands openly condemned before God, for whether it be "the Jews, because they fulfilled the law only according only to its letter", or "the heathen, because they fulfilled the law only in part and not at all according to its spirit." [17]

Furthermore, as "nothing in all the vast universe can come to pass otherwise than God has eternally purposed," [18] God does sometimes remove His restraint in order to show forth the depravity of natural man along with our absolute dependence upon Him to redeem for "the Law gives occasion to sin unless there is the assistance of divine grace, and the heart, mind and will are divinely directed toward keeping the law." Yet, "wherever the Law prevails, man is moved (*by it*), to sin more than he is to fulfill it." [19]

Such a prevailing spirit of wickedness through the "deceitfulness of sin" (Hebrews 3:13), must surely identify this present age towards that of end times for Satan, who will be held accountable, is ever increasingly breaking down this hold of law and order through the agency and pride of man. The self-will of man will also be held accountable, "all of these evil things come from within, and defile the man" (Mark 7:23).

Undeniably have God's ethical and moral standards been crumbled, derided and held as meaningless by a society where century old laws have been uprooted and changed at will. For example, the ordinance for marriage was given at creation for the preservation of the world of mankind, as our Lord says, "For this cause shall a man leave father and mother, and shall cleave to his wife...Wherefore they are no more twain but one flesh. What therefore God hath joined together, let no man asunder" (Matthew 19:5-6). However, this blessed institution has been torn asunder by many countries where homosexuality is normalized and legislated for.

---

[17] Martin Luther, ibid., p. 58.
[18] A.W Pink, *The Sovereignty of God*, ibid., p.43.
[19] Martin Luther, ibid., p. 59.

And even those that do consider the spiritual there is a myriad of darkness as seen by polytheism and the innumerable number of false heathen gods down the centuries of time, all of which hold no true moral fulfillment or value before God. Satan's abyss is very dark yet believers in Christ can see through this veneer and know that Christ has ultimate control and victory in the course of this world, for which Satan can never overcome or outmaneuver His sovereign will in salvation: -

> "and he doeth according to his will in the army of heaven, and among the inhabitants of the earth: and none can stay his hand, or say unto him, What doest thou?" (Daniel 4:35).

SATAN'S RESTRAINT: -

Outside of Grace, however, Satan continues unfazed to vex, antagonize, meddle and confuse truth so as to hold any line of darkness possible. Natural man is thus hedged about, "O Lord, I know that the way of man is not in himself: it is not in man that walketh to direct his steps" (Jeremiah 10:23).

But the following passage provides great insight into Satan's permitted scope of operation: -

6. "And I saw an angel come down from heaven, having the key of the bottomless pit and great chain in his hand. And he laid hold on the dragon, that old serpent, which is the Devil, and Satan, and bound him a thousand years. And cast him into the bottomless pit and shut him up, and set a seal upon him that he should deceive the nations no more, till the thousand years should be fulfilled: and after that he must be loosed a little season" (Revelation 20:1-3).

There is such a mix of erroneous conclusion(s) from these

verses, which is ironic for this passage essentially describes Satan's limited restraint or suspended sentence by which he is currently held in check since our Savior's death. But the real context must be looked upon as the thousand years representing God's full amount of time for the present Gospel age as determined from Christ's first coming to that extending to the time of His second advent. "Satan's influence on earth is curtailed so that he is unable to prevent the extension of the church among the nations by means of an active missionary programme." [20] Satan's restraint is also suggested by our Lord, "how else can one enter a strong man's house, and spoil his goods, unless he first bind the strong man" (Matthew 12:29). This strong man is Satan and Christ's Gospel of truth spoils his house.

The Apostle Paul was bound when was he was sent to Jerusalem "not knowing what things would befall him there" (Acts 20:22); The Lord also healed the women from her bond on the Sabbath day, "whom Satan hath bound, lo, these eighteen years" (Luke 13:16). So bound in this sense means that Satan as a spiritual being is not immobile but is still able to move and function and roam, but not to the full extent and scope that he would like. Satan's binding is also seen in two other ways. Firstly, by his failure to devour the Man Child "as soon as it was born," (Revelation 12:4) and, secondly, by his failure to both destroy and tarnish our Lord's mission in going to the Calvary's Cross in the temptation of Christ at the start of His earthly ministry (Luke 4:1-13).

The analogy of a raging and vicious dog on a chain provides a good example for Satan would destroy the church if possible but for the Lord's overall redemptive purpose in this world which is to bring glory to Himself through the salvation of His elect who

---

[20] W. J Grier, *The Momentous Event,* Banner of Truth Trust, first Published 1948, reprinted 2013, p. 115.

are to burn as bright lights amidst such darkness, "and be set on a candlestick" (Mark 4:21).

END TIMES: -

Even at end times, Christ has ultimate control, for as Scripture fully predicts His second advent, Satan too, who is a great imitator of Christ, must have a similar counterpart, where the Apostle Paul teaches that anti-Christ will be revealed, "that man of sin" who is called the wicked one, or "the son of perdition" (2 Thessalonians 2:3). This manifestation will no doubt magnify all human power and reasoning that it will appear to eclipse Christ's divine dominion and power. Such antagonism is evident today where scientific humanism is given all manner of authority and credence in deceiving the nations against God, as seen in Daniel's prophetic reference to the "little horn" (Daniel 7:8). Satan's subtle influence holds sway over society, "And he shall speak great words against the most High, and shall wear out the saints of the most High" (Daniel 7:25).

Moral standards have also been comprehensively derided, "For the mystery of iniquity doth already work" yet this spirit and manifestation of anti-Christ is only ever reactionary to Christ's eternal plans, "only he who now letteth will let, until he be taken out of the way" (2 Thessalonians 2:7) This is seen in three ways: -

First, when anti-Christ shall manifest himself at the end of this age, "the king shall do according to his will; and he shall exalt himself, and shall magnify himself above every god, and shall speak marvelous things against the God of gods, and shall prosper until the indignation be accomplished: for that that is determined shall be done" (Daniel 11:36). Satan's little season is determined for the purpose of purifying His people by much persecution and tribulation before our Lord's return, "Blessed are they that are persecuted for righteousness sake: for theirs is the kingdom of heaven" (Matthew 5:10).

The period of tribulation is also seen by the two witnesses who are 'overcome and killed' after finishing their testimony by "the beast that ascendeth out of the bottomless pit" who "shall make war against them" (Revelation 11:7). Christian witness, both corporate and personal, has provoked the deaths of countless martyrs for the faith right throughout the history of the church. So is Revelation a book of comfort for believers and martyrs alike who will share the ultimate and spiritual victory as those quickened in Christ against the judgment of all ungodliness and the seed of the serpent. The church militant is now robed in triumph: –

> "And after three days and a half the Spirit of life from God entered into them, and they stood upon their feet; and great fear fell upon them which saw them. And they heard a great voice from heaven saying Come up hither...and their enemies beheld them" (Revelation 11:11-12).

Second, we see in the Apostle John's further vision of end time events, the manifestation of Satan's unrestrained season with the innumerable forces of heathenism, as represented by "Gog and Magog" (Revelation 20:8) gathered out of her far distant territories, united to compass "the camp of the saints about, and the beloved city" (Revelation 20:9) or the true nation of God. Yet this determined and bitter period of assault and antagonism is entirely within Christ's control for we see in John's preceding vision of the same event even the enemies of Christ turning upon themselves to make the whore desolate, "and shall eat her flesh and burn her with fire. For God hath put in their hearts to fulfil his will, and to agree...until the words of God be fulfilled" (Revelation 17:16-17). How final and complete shall divine vengeance be as the arms of heathenism and worldliness are totally and utterly broken: –

"Alas, alas, that great city Babylon, that mighty
city! for in one hour is thy judgment come"
(Revelation 18:10).

Third, after "that Wicked be revealed" the Lord will consume
anti-Christ with "the spirit of his mouth, and shall destroy by the
brightness of his coming" (2 Thessalonians 2:8). Yet prior to
this consummation, God magnifies the deception of anti-Christ
by sending "a strong delusion, that they should believe a lie" (2
Thessalonians 2:11). Just as with the unbelieving Jews of old, God
will in effect withdraw His Grace and give the unregenerate over
in damnation to themselves and their perpetual unbelief.

Such a strong delusion to believe a lie permeates today with
the theory of evolution which holds a vice like grip over western
society and forms the base of much godless humanistic and secular
thought. Natural selection has given rise to much evil including
the Holocaust itself and modern day cohabitation and fornication.
Atheism now follows, which is a religion and belief system in itself
to deny the existence of God and our divine Creator.

The Lord's determined period of Grace will close once His
sovereign purpose in saving all of His elect is fulfilled, whereby,
the souls outside of Grace must face judgment. The will of
God's decree supremely governs the affairs of this world which
leaves Satan totally defeated and waging a losing and restricted
battle since his judgment was pronounced in Genesis 3:15. He
was completely defeated by our Savior's death at Calvary where
He took authority over death, and now, Satan and his followers,
"where the beast and the false prophet are," (Revelation 20:10)
will face their eternal sentence and torture in the lake of fire.

The final punishment of Satan, however, coincides with the
unmistakable last trumpet of our Lord's return. This, in turn,
heralds the signal for seven other simultaneous events. (Please
note, God infinite is in no way limited by time or space but is from

our earthly and finite capacity that a sequence has been placed on
the events that follow): -

1. Both the just and unjust will be raised as described by
   Daniel, after the tribulation, that "time of trouble...
   and at that time thy people shall be delivered, every one
   that shall be found written in the book. And many of
   them that sleep in the dust of the earth shall awake, some
   to everlasting life and some to shame and everlasting
   contempt" (Daniel 12:1-2). These join together with those
   that remain physically alive on earth at our Lord's second
   coming, which will be a literal, visible and bodily coming.
2. The saints, or those justified in Christ and alive at the
   time, will be raptured to meet the Lord in the air and
   given new bodies. This rapture is portrayed as a snatching
   away to join those saints that have slept since their first
   resurrection at conversion who will descend with the Lord
   and also be given new bodies, "the dead shall be raised
   incorruptible, we shall be changed" (1 Corinthians 15:52).
   The great marriage supper of the Lamb perfectly begins
   with His people escorting the King to the earth, both
   those newly raised from the dead and those that remain
   alive at the time of His return.
3. Despite the Bible indicating that non believers will also be
   given resurrected bodies on the last day, "fear Him who
   can destroy both body and soul in hell" (Matthew 10:28),
   the glorious unification of Christ's visible and invisible
   church will be in full view of the unjust, but, marvel as
   they may at this spectacle, mourning and sorrow will
   follow, "and then shall all the tribes of the earth mourn"
   (Matthew 24:30). The time of salvation is over with the
   door upon Grace now sealed, and those that remain
   outside will forever remain, for: -

4. Eternal separation is now set before the judgment throne of Christ comprising of a massive audience of every person since Adam with the "sheep on right hand, but the goats on the left" (Matthew 25:33). Every knee shall bow and acknowledge Him as Lord, as all eternal destinies are now sealed in the most significant scene in world history, "And I saw the dead, small and great, stand before God and the books were opened, and another book was opened which is the book of life, and the dead were judged out of those things that were written in the books" (Revelation 20:12). Known as the Great White Throne Judgment, this is the judgment the unbelievers must face.

Scripture also confirms itself as a simultaneous judgment for both the just and unjust "will both grow together until the harvest" (Matthew 13:30). The unjust are gathered first, "As therefore the tares are gathered and burned in the fire; so shall it be in the end of this world" (Matthew 13:40). Then shall the righteous shine forth as the sun in the kingdom of their Father. Who hath ears to hear, let him hear" (Matthew 13:43).

5. Immediately following judgment, the wicked are then cast into hell at the same time the the last enemy is abolished. "Since both events take place at the time of the second death, then both events must of necessity take place at one and the same time. Things equal to the same thing are equal to one another." [21] Thus are the unjust, along with death and hell cast into the burning lake of fire, "This is the second death" (Revelation 20:14).

6. Finally, with all wickedness thus removed, the final and everlasting state is now consummated before God the Father in a new heaven and new earth, "wherein dwelleth

---

[21] William E Cox, ibid., p. 108.

righteousness" (2 Peter 3:13). "Sin will no longer exist outside of hell." [22]

7. At consummation, Christ will also hand over His current office as mediator to the God Father as all of the host of His elect will now be in glory forever more, "then shall the Son also himself be subject unto him that put all things under him, that God maybe all in all" (1 Corinthians 15:28); "And ye are Christ's; and Christ is God's" (1 Corinthians 3:23). "He will no longer rule over the universe as mediator, but only as God; while headship over His people is to continue for ever." [23]

As we shall next consider, Satan is certainly defeated but his darkened influence most certainly pervades this current Gospel age.

---

[22] Ibid., p. 93.

[23] W.J Grier, ibid., p. 77.

CHAPTER 3

SATAN'S INFLUENCE

God's decrees are certain and it is from His eternal prescience, or foreknowledge, that determines His will. It is infallible as He worketh nothing by chance or accidentally, as "the will of God is represented in Scripture as the final cause of all things." [24] Divine providence is always fulfilled irrespective of any contingent actions, inclinations, or co-operation from the creatures' inferior cause, as Joseph declares to his brethren, "But as for you, ye thought evil against me; but God meant it unto good, to bring to pass, as it is this day, to save much people alive" (Genesis 50:20). David also affirms that nothing is unforeseen or unexpected before the Lord, who: –

> "bringeth the counsel of the heathen to nought:
> he maketh the devices of the people of none effect.
> The counsel of the Lord standeth for ever, the
> thoughts of his heart to all generations" (Psalm
> 33:10-11).

Yet God is not the author of sin any more than a lawgiver, who gives the law he knows people will break and transgress, is

---

[24] Louis Berkhof, *A Summary of Christian Doctrine*, The Banner of Truth Trust, 1960, p. 32.

guilty of giving the law. God allows things to happen, it is His permissive will, but He does not condone them. God withdraws His restraining hand and so man hardens his own heart to Satan's trickery and deception of sin, "The transgression of the wicked saith within my heart, that there is no fear of God before his eyes"(Psalm 36:1).

"While they sit backward to God's precepts, they row forward to his decrees; his decrees to permit their sin, and to punish them for their sin permitted." [25] In this sense, they are ever moving forward to God's righteous decree in judgment for "the greater God's long-suffering is, the greater also will be His judgment if His goodness is bestowed in vain." [26] "But after thy hardness and impenitent heart treasurest up unto thyself wrath against the day of wrath and revelation of the righteous judgment of God" (Romans 2:5).

REPROBATE: -

Although God's sovereign purpose can be served through the unregenerate as Pharoah's abuse of the Israelites shows, where God punished him so that he could not repent, "For the scripture saith unto Pharaoh, Even for this same purpose have I raised thee up, that I might shew my power in thee, and that my name might be declared throughout all the earth" (Romans 9:17). Similarly, many years later, was Gentile King Cyrus chosen to advance the work of restoring the temple after the captivity (Ezra 1:1-2), who along with Judas, in betraying our Savior, both served God's sovereign purpose: –

> "For to do whatsoever thy hand and thy counsel
> determined before to be done" (Acts 4:28).

---

[25] Thomas Watson, ibid., p. 70.
[26] Martin Luther, ibid., p. 54.

The reprobate, however, as powerless and poisoned by sin, are permitted to damn themselves for it is they who stubbornly resist and disobey the moral duty of God's known will and mandates as revealed through the law and the Gospel. Carnal and reprobate minds, as given over to the earnest of damnation through the pleasures of this world, "to do those things that are not convenient" (Romans 1:28) along with Satan's ceaseless activity since the fall, have both combined to build many layers of deception, misery, and vanity.

Evil forces such as the beast "of the sea" (Revelation 13:1) and the false prophet from "the earth" (Revelation 13:11) have all combined to create strongholds which deceptively influence this world's systems of government and education that match the already innumerable number of cults and false religions. These changes are set after periods of much campaigning for the spirit of anti-Christ elevates the pride of man where he shall "think to change times and laws" (Daniel 7:25).

Secular society has many false gods to dazzle and bewilder the ungodly down a darkened path. Entertainment is a tool where Elvis for example, still holds a cult following worldwide. The Beatles also held countless in their sway as the permissive society began its moral decline to its exponentially worse state of ethical and anti-values that prevails today. Many countries have leading soap and television personalities who lead a great 'self-esteem' type movement and generation, which incite both lust and covetousness to fill the void of life without God. Timothy warns of such temptation and snare, and falling into many foolish and hurtful lusts, "which drown men in destruction and perdition" (1 Timothy 6:9).

Satan's great strength is observation, cunning along with an ability to subjugate, direct and corral the great and busy mass of secular society into a false sense of security. Most are like sheep who have gone astray and follow the fashions of this world through the rationale that as everybody else is doing likewise, everything must be fine, despite it being the wrong way that is actually leading to everlasting ruin. "How many by the wind of popular breath have been blown to hell! Whom the devil cannot destroy by intemperance, he does by vainglory." [27]

Sport as a further example of a popular and secular god has reached disproportionate levels of following and performing on the back of corporate sponsorships where sporting success and individual sporting achievements are endlessly flaunted. So much so that the truth of God is changed into a lie: –

> "and worshipped and served the creature more than the Creator, who is blessed forevermore. Amen" (Romans 1:25).

The fallacy of agnosticism also justifies much ungodly behavior because in neither admitting nor dismissing the existence of God, a god of our own making is thus created. If nothing can be proven or disproven then, the existence of a higher power, such as a god, must be so far away in space and time that people can essentially act as they like before making a hopeful and welcome meeting with such a god at death; "And with all deceivableness of unrighteousness in them that perish; because they received not the love of the truth, that they might be saved" (2 Thessalonians 2:10).

Consider also the particular functions of this secular world and a downturn in the world economy for instance will have people on edge at one another which will turn the world's media, another "snare of the devil" awash with conspiracy, "who are taken captive by him at his will" (2 Timothy 2:26). All of this concludes that "Satan contrives nothing with greater care than to adulterate, with every possible corruption, the pure invocation of

---

[27] Thomas Watson, ibid., p. 23.

God, or to draw us away from the only God to the invocation of the creatures." [28]

Sensuality is a typical method of temptation, "For all that is in the world, the lust of the flesh, and the lust of the eyes, and the pride of life is not of the Father, but is of the world" (1 John 2:16). This tri-fold of carnal worship is subjective in that feelings are the primary and determining factor for what is deemed as right or wrong. If it makes 'me' or even others around 'me' happy then this must be right, a thought which is devoid of any objective standing upon God's Word and has very little empathy for others around as it centers around self.

Satan has set man firmly on his pedestal from which everything does gravitate, and although this is not a study of social issues as a whole, it is reasonable to see, from a Biblical perspective, why mental illness has become so prevalent for nothing is substantial to fill the void of life that remains without God. God's Word, of course, confounds such vanity: –

> "All nations are before him as nothing; and they
> are counted to him less than nothing, and vanity"
> (Isaiah 40:17).

A further line of attack that is pitched particularly against young school-age children is the transgender meddling of God's distinct order for male and female where one can choose their gender based purely on feelings and emotion, for which schools themselves foster such activity. "That God made us male and female (Genesis 1:27), not an alphabet soup of genders. The modern gender bending ideology is ultimately an attack on God's plan and purpose for us and for the flourishing of human beings." [29]

---

[28] John Calvin *Commentary on Genesis*, Banner of Truth, 1965, vol 1, p. 223.
[29] Creation Ministries Extra, *Whence the craziness enveloping the once-Christian west*, June 2018.

Abortion is legalized in many countries worldwide but the fundamental question still remains as to whether man has ultimate control to determine life? The Bible, as God's ultimate authority, places this control with our Creator, "So God created mankind in his own image, in the image of God he created them, male and female he created them,' (Genesis 1:27); "Children are a heritage from the Lord, offspring a reward from him" (Psalm 127:3); "For you created my inmost being, you knit me together in my mother's womb. I praise you because I am fearfully and wonderfully made" (Psalm 139:13-14). The other end of life has several countries where euthanasia is legalized, for which the same Biblical principle of pro-life must also apply to determine the outcome of life.

Society does appease its conscience somewhat in bringing some important issues to bear like poverty, domestic violence, along with various health issues and charitable organizations etc. But this is ultimately flawed in that the foundational problem of sin is not even remotely considered and is also unbalanced given the reality that abortion is legislated for in most western countries.

THE BELIEVERS' BATTLE WITHIN: -

Satan's dominion towards such moral degradation must surely point towards end times, "This know also, that in the last days perilous times shall come" (2 Timothy 3:1). Each perilous season, however, "shall wax worse and worse, deceiving and being deceived" (2 Timothy 3:13) until the end of time.

Satan though, continues his tirade and rage from within man as well, through the continual tempting and leading of souls towards sin for both believers, who are supposedly spiritually discerned, and unbelievers alike who are spiritually blind. It is to the believer though that Satan does pay particular attention to morally draw them aside and into sin for the pull of the flesh against the Spirit is what the Apostle Paul laments, "for what I do I allow not; but what I hate, that do I" (Romans 7:15). It is a relentless battle for which every believer is sorely tried.

Over a long period, Satan plays on the battle weariness of a believer by his continual cunning, conniving and plotting against to draw such moral lapse for which we must remain prayerfully alert. The pull of the flesh and indwelling sin is the real spiritual battle that all believers are engaged to overcome for Grace itself is young glory; Grace is glory in the bud. "The point we need to see is the state of grace is nearer to the state of glory than it is to the state of sin.

Believers are nearer in character to God and the angels than they are to unregenerate and lost sinners. The moral good that they will is greater than the evil which they do." [30] Growth, thereby, is the increase in degree, size, strength, vigor, and power of the Graces which the Holy Spirit plants in the heart of every believer, "Grow in grace, and in the knowledge of our Lord and Saviour Jesus Christ" (2 Peter 3:18).

But perhaps the greatest blend of pressure from within and wicked forces against, must come down to the nuclear family for there is immense external pressure on a modern day family to provide income to survive. The Lord, of course, will provide for His own, but provision must still be made to keep the household afloat, and financial pressure is a constant threat faced by families both inside and outside of Grace every day, to complicate and often pre-determine our mindset.

Then there are the daily challenges of running a Godly household, amidst the busyness of work coupled with school runs and after school activities etc. Many believing households in becoming so earthbound and pre-occupied lose sight of eternal reality to bear fruit and just get swept forward with the hustle and bustle of the world as Satan would prefer. Many do not grow in Grace for which the third seed of the sower from Mark 4:19 does

---

[30] Maurice Roberts, *The Thought Of God*, Banner of Truth Trust, 1993, p. 98.

apply, "And the cares of this world, and the deceitfulness of riches, and the lusts of other things entering in, choke the word, and it becometh unfruitful." But is this really the standard for believers today? Should not believers, endowed with such blessings of the Spirit and answered prayer from God's throne above, ingest God's Word more fully for a much higher fruitfulness: -

> "such as hear the word, and receive it, and bring forth fruit, some thirtyfold, some sixty, and some an hundred" (Mark 4:20).

Further confusion surrounds the role of male headship within the family as males are quite often portrayed as sidelined or watered down figures throughout western society, lacking any real and significant authority. The lead, in turn, often goes to the mother who is seen to be the main authority by which all major decisions are made. Biblically, however, fathers still maintain headship of the family since the fall, "Unto the woman he said, I will greatly multiply thy sorrow and thy conception; in sorrow thou shalt bring forth children; and thy desire shall be to thy husband, and he shall rule over thee" (Genesis 3:16). Fatherhood is, therefore, such a vital role within the nuclear family, which too often breaks down, leaving children from families both inside and outside of Grace vulnerable to Satan's attacks and directive. The foundation of society as a whole is stripped back amidst such volatility and uncertainty and has now reached disproportionate levels as a true sign of hardship since the fall which may only be relieved at consummation in the "new heavens and a new earth, wherein dwelleth righteousness" (2 Peter 3:13).

Satan, however, is also an accuser of our brethren before God who is upon His throne. Although, as a mark of restraint, Satan needed permission to test Job, "And the Lord said unto Satan, Behold, he is in thine hand; but save his life" (Job 2:6), he still does have full access to God's throne room above. After he has encroached a believer into sin, he thus uses this access to accuse the Christian of condemnation for such transgression and iniquity, "which accused them before our God day and night" (Revelation 12:10). As seen from heaven, Satan was present in the conversion of Joshua the High Priest, "and Satan standing at his right hand to resist him" (Zechariah 3:1).

Satan, as a spirit, does have access and vantage over all the earth "And the Lord said unto Satan, whence comest thou? Then Satan answered and said unto the Lord, from going to and fro in the earth, from walking up and down in it," (Job 1:7). There is nothing in man that he cannot observe which makes the person of Satan a very formidable being once fully seen in all of his darkened and wicked context for his wrath is great and is fervently energized given the relatively short time left in which has to operate. Yet overall, believer's must remember that Satan is but an instrument in the overall sovereign redemptive purpose of God which is to bring glory to Himself and bear true light amongst such ruinous darkness, "is not this a brand plucked out of the fire?" (Zechariah 3:2).

HIGHER CRITICISM: -

Another vital aspect to consider is Satan's sustained attack on the Bible's authority and the inerrancy of Scripture. Theological liberalism began in earnest back in the 1850s when various theologians from Germany started to attack the Bible's inerrancy and infallibility, known as "higher criticism." Such liberal thought, which represents an open mindedness and tolerance towards Biblical doctrine and historic Christian beliefs, quickly spread throughout Europe and had gained support in the USA by the second half of the nineteenth century.

A lower view of Scripture has been the result for "liberals held that the Bible, while it contains God's word, is not without error, and so it must be read just like any other book; its historic context must be interpreted through critical analysis." [31] It "is rooted in a desire to dethrone God and destroy the Protestant faith from within the church. The pride of man again succumbed to Satan's ploy as the higher critics were scholars who attempted to use their intellectual ability to argue that the Bible contained many errors, and therefore was not infallible." [32]

Interpreting Scripture through critical analysis is subjective and is devoid any serious consideration of God's divine authorship. Genesis for example, when taken in a mythical or poetic sense, fails to grasp crucial theological principles like original sin and the depravity of man from which the rest of Scripture does follow. "The ideas of higher criticism developed in an era dominated by evolutionary thought, and were profoundly influenced by the philosophy of the Enlightenment (an eighteenth century movement which elevated human reason to the place of the final arbiter of truth) ...In theology, the scientific study of the Scriptures produced not God's thoughts about man but man's thoughts about God." [33]

Flawed theological ideas like theistic evolution that allows Christians to believe in both creation and evolution have since followed. Open Theism is further thought that tarnish God's decrees as of acts irrevocably finished, and draws the conclusion that "God does know everything to be known, but he does not know the future." [34] Such temporal and inconclusive thought elevates man's free will, in that "the elect may become reprobates, and the reprobates elect." [35] This robs God of His power and glory in sovereignly determining and saving His own, and proves

[31] E. S Williams, *Holistic Mission*, ibid., p. 36.

[32] E. S Williams, ibid., p. 47.

[33] E. S Williams, ibid., p. 34.

[34] *What is open theism?* https://www.gotquestions.org/open-theism.html, (accessed July 24 2018).

[35] The Works of John Owen, Vol. 5, *A Display of Arminianism*, https://www. puritanlibrary.com, p. 60, (accessed September 14, 2018).

Satan's eagerness to both deride the authority and infallibility of Scripture along with the supremacy of God in foreknowing all things, against which the Apostle implores: –

> "O Timothy, keep that which is committed to thy trust, avoiding profane and vain babblings, and oppositions of science falsely so called" (1 Timothy 6:20).

Satan's attack on God's Word carries forward to the acceptance of textual criticism from the original New Testament manuscripts. The Jewish Bible, or the Old Testament, were originally written almost entirely in Hebrew, with some parts in Aramaic. A Greek version of the Hebrew canon was completed in the 3rd century A.D., known as the Septuagint, with St Jerome's Latin translation of both Testaments completed shortly after. Known as the Vulgate, this "became the standard of Western Christianity for a thousand years or more." [36]

It wasn't until the 15th century when Dutch theologian Desiderius Erasmus published an edition of the New Testament containing the Greek text and his own translation into Latin from hand copied Greek manuscripts, known as the 'Received Text.' To eliminate previous textual errors, 2 revised versions were subsequently printed in 1527 and 1535 and both Martin Luther and William Tyndale translated the Scriptures into their vernacular language using the same Greek text. "In Germany, Luther produced the first complete translation from the original Greek and Hebrew into a modern European language. His German language translation of the New Testament was published in 1522 and that of the complete Bible in 1534; this

---

[36] Encyclopedia Britannica, *Biblical Translation*, https://www.britannica.com/topic/biblical-translation, (accessed October 31, 2018).

remained the official Bible for German Protestants and was the basis for Danish, Swedish, and other translations." [37]

Tyndale's translation of the New Testament and part of the Old from between 1525-1535 became a model for a series of subsequent English translations, including the abiding King James Version (KJV) of 1611. All of these translations are based upon the 'Received Text,' or the 'Textus Receptus,' which became the dominant Greek text of the New Testament for the following two hundred and fifty years by which God did faithfully preserve His Word.

It was not until the publication of the Westcott and Hort Greek New Testament in 1881 that the Textus Receptus lost its favored position in translation. The 'critical text' used to produce the New Testament in Greek as it became known, is now the standard Greek text used for modern interpretation and translation. With the exception of the New King James Version that was inaugurated in 1975 with aim of updating the vocabulary and grammar of the original KJV, much of the compromised and worldly church of today use modern translations that emanate from this critical text.

A proliferation of Bible versions are now in circulation from the New American Standard Version, the English Standard Version, the Revised Standard Version, the New International Version, New Living Translation through to the New English Bible, all of which have slowly deviated and moved away from the original and intended meaning. As per Satan's tact, such easy and watered down translations that do not challenge their readers, have all undermined God's Word and helped lead the church into compromise and upholding false doctrine. Sadly, many congregations do not hold enough discernment to, first of all, recognize error and, secondly, to then hold their pastors accountable against such error.

---

[37] Encyclopedia Britannica, *Biblical Translation*, ibid.

INTERPRETATION: -

Finally, another area where Satan has ensnared and drawn man into confusion is through interpretation of Scripture. There have been many wonderful and varied interpretations concerning end time theology alone throughout the ages, yet the following section is aimed at providing some overall guidance and methodology of interpretation. As the Bible is like no other book, the Scriptures, thereby, demand more upon its readers than any other does, for it is divinely written with a divine intent for man to study in humility and to lay open accurately: -

> "rightly dividing the word of truth" (2 Timothy 2:15).

It is a great systematic and organizing principle of Scripture that runs right throughout the Bible, the theme of the spiritual against the worldly and ungodly for in the eternal realm only those souls ordained and born of God have life with everything else, justly, facing eternal ruin and death.

Essentially, therefore, Scripture can be drawn into two distinct and eternal realms;

1. The spiritual realm represents the Godly who are justified to inherit everlasting life through Jesus Christ, and
2. The ungodly realm represents this carnal world that will draw a wage of death from sin (Romans 6:23).

Context is crucial to correct biblical exegesis and hermeneutics to prevent both error and misunderstanding for which there is both an internal and external context;

The internal context of the passage are considerations like: -

i. The literal meaning of the passage and what it actually says.

ii. Grammatical is the immediate sentence and paragraph within which a word or phrase is found.

iii. Outline then determines the structure of the book, followed by the chapter and paragraph itself. The structures of Ezekiel and Daniel, for example, are not only historical narratives during Israel's captivity but are also Prophetic concerning God's future plans for His covenant people, or true Israel, along with His dealings with unrepentant Israelites (discussed more fully chapter 6).

iv. The analogy of faith represents a synthesis and the comparison with parts and other related passages in Scripture. This is crucial with Prophesy to garner the correct overall sense of Scripture, particularly with Old Testament (OT) Prophesy correctly aligning with the conclusion from similar and related New Testament (NT) passages.

The external context to the passage are considerations like: -

v. The historical, cultural and geographical background, which will help identify to whom the passage is addressed and how it was understood at the time.

Principles of truth can emanate from single verses, like the Holy character and justice of God which are consistent throughout Scripture, yet from an interpretive perspective we learn more as we read from the OT to NT, for the NT always clarifies the framework of God's redemptive purpose for mankind that was established in the OT. It is not that OT believers knew nothing of Christ, but rather that their knowledge and understanding of Him was quite limited, or veiled. Topics such as eschatology and rules for practical Christian living are also clarified in the NT, for which we do not go to the OT to understand something in finality as the NT always provides greater lucidity.

God's revelation is progressive so we learn more of God's providence by His arrangement and collection of books, letters, and texts. The NT, thereby, confirms the foundations laid from the OT for it is the foundation that points forward in various pictures, types, and shadows to what Christ does accomplish in the NT. We can't ignore either Testament if we are to be equipped in full knowledge of righteousness, particularly as the essence of the Gospel through the framework of grace is so readily found throughout the OT.

Scripture will always interpret itself for which sound doctrine emanates from reading the whole Bible, not just part, or from an isolated verse or passage in a singular, or 'hyper-literal,' context. (A hyper-literal interpretation puts a veil over Scripture by not considering the symbolic and spiritual sense of Prophesy from many books including Daniel, Ezekiel, and Revelation: -

"And he sent and signified it by his angel unto his servant John" (Revelation 1:1).

(The word *signified* thus sets the tone for the rest of the book of Revelation as a book of symbolic meaning and interpretation).

The analogy of faith, which draws a conclusion from other and similar parts of Scripture, ensures that the correct interpretation of a single text is coherent with our understanding of the whole of Scripture. The widely revealed truths of Scripture declared in doctrinal statements and historical confessions, which validate the majority sense for a current period, also prevents turning Scripture on its head from singular verse(s) or passage(s).

Prayerfully, we are to ask for illumination of Christ by the Spirit for a fuller knowledge and revelation is the challenge of every believer in sustaining a greater alignment and obedience to His Word: -

"Teach me, O Lord, the way of thy statutes; and I
shall keep it unto the end" (Psalm 119:33).

"The revelation of Scripture closed long ago, the Bible being
a complete revelation of all that we need to know about God, and
about how believers should live their lives. God may guide us
personally by enlightening us about the meaning of Scripture,
but he does not add new doctrine." [38] Despite any new revelation
ceasing to mankind as a whole, as Satan has led various sects
to believe otherwise, like Mormonism which errantly trace their
origin back to certain visions of Joseph Smith in the 1820s.

Thus are many drawn aside from walking in the true light
of God's Word for "as a child may spell out letters and learn
to pronounce words which he appertains, so may we ascertain
the literal or grammatical meaning this Word and yet have no
spiritual knowledge of it, and thus belong to that generation of
whom it is said "hearing ye shall hear, and shall not understand;
and seeing ye shall see, and shall not perceive" (Matt. 13: 14).
"There is a veil of pride which effectually prevents us from seeing
ourselves in the mirror of the Word." [39]

The Apostle Paul right throughout his instructional, doctrinal
and non-symbolic letters and Epistles like Romans, Galatians,
Colossians, and Ephesians, designates his Words as Spirit-taught
words, "Which things also we speak, not in the words which man's
wisdom teacheth, but which the Holy Ghost teacheth; comparing
spiritual things with spiritual" (1 Corinthians 2:13). Therefore,
a good working rule to follow is that a literal interpretation of
Prophesy is to be accepted unless: -

---

[38] Robin Compston, *God or Mammon? The Snare of the Prosperity Gospel*,
Wakeman Trust London, 2018, p. 13.
[39] A.W. Pink, *Interpretation of the Scriptures*, Baker Book House Company,
1972, p. 9.

"(a) the passages contain obvious figurative language, or (b) unless the New Testament gives authority for interpreting them in other than a literal sense, or (c) unless a literal interpretation would produce a contradiction with truths, principles, or factual statements contained in non-symbolic books of the New Testament. Another obvious rule to follow is that the clearest New Testament passages in non-symbolic books are to be the norm for the interpretation of Prophesy, rather than obscure or partial revelations contained in the Old Testament." [40]

SPHERES: -

Finally, particular spheres also run throughout Scripture which pertains to each realm. The spiritual realm has various spheres including promise, light, righteous, faith, belief, prayer, obedience, justified, repentant, forgiveness, regenerate, holy, sanctified, saved, free, grace, life, and heaven, all of which direct the thoughts of believers throughout the ages heavenward. Faith in God's promise, for example, is what persuaded Noah's obedience to firstly build the ark and then to enter along with his family, "And Noah did according unto all that the Lord commanded him" (Genesis 7:5).

King Manasseh's impenitence during his early years as King of Judah, drew the wrath of the Lord that led him to be taken captive by the Assyrians. Yet amidst his affliction, he truly sought forgiveness, "And prayed unto him...Then Manasseh knew that the Lord he was God" (2 Chronicles 33:13). Back in Jerusalem, his repentance pervaded throughout all of Judah, "And he repaired the altar of the Lord, and sacrificed thereon peace offerings and

---

[40] William E Cox, ibid., pp. 24-25.

thank offerings, and commanded Judah to serve the Lord God of Israel" (2 Chronicles 33:16). Thus is true repentance so powerful and life changing for all of God's people.

The ungodly realm represents Satan's earthly and carnal domain, is drawn in total opposition to the spiritual, and includes spheres such as damnation, dark, unrighteous, unbelief, rebellion, unjustified, unrepentant, obstinate, unregenerate, unholy, unsanctified, unsaved, bond, works, death, and hell. The Spirit will often use these as warnings as awakenings to sinners in directing to life in Christ, like the parable of the prodigal son in Luke 15:11-32 where through the lure of money, the son enters a period, or sphere, of rebellion. His riotous living then leads him into poverty before he comes to himself, which then, in turn, drives him back to his gracious father who does receive him back with open arms.

Primarily, the spiritual or ungodly realm is determined by identifying the contextual nature of the passage being considered, whether it is historical or prophetic etc. This can then be compared to other related passages, with similar themes or spheres of Scripture for the analogy of faith. In Galatians 4:28-31 for instance, the Apostle uses an allegory comprising of the spheres of bond against the free to determine the children of promise from Genesis 21. The Lord cast the bondwomen Hagar and her son Ishmael out of Abraham's family to remove the breach and reveal the Lord's sovereign will, "for in Isaac shall thy seed be called" (Genesis 21:12).

Ishmael was the embodiment of a carnal solution in providing an heir, "And Sarai said unto Abram, Behold now, the Lord has restrained me from bearing: I pray thee, go in unto my maid; it may be that I may obtain children by her" (Genesis 16:2). It also showed disloyalty to God's promises made to Abraham in the proceeding chapter but the greater picture is that only the true spiritual seed shall inherit the everlasting blessings and privileges of God's house by Grace. Conversely, the children of the bondwomen shall not inherit the blessing, for inheritance is not of the law, neither are they heirs who are of the works to it (legalism).

Scripture can also be given in a primary or secondary sense for which context will determine the most suitable meaning. The word "tempt" for example primarily signifies to make trial of, to prove, to test. Secondarily, it signifies to allure, seduce, or solicit to evil. Manifestly the word "tempt" is not used in the same sense in those sentences for it has a spiritual application in that the Lord will often try His people, "that God did tempt Abraham" (Genesis 22:1), but God does permit Satan to tempt His people as well, "let no man say when he is tempted, I am tempted of God" (James 1:13).

A singular view on either passage may not lead to a correct understanding. "When Satan tempts he places an allurement before us with the object of encompassing our downfall; but when God tempts or tests us, He has our welfare at heart. Every trial is thus a temptation, for it serves to make manifest the prevailing disposition of the heart - whether it be holy or unholy." [41]

THE SUM OF SATANIC ACTIVITY: -

Although the Lord's sovereign purpose of redemption cannot be prevented, the sum of Satanic activity can be asserted as follows: - Before the fall, Satan beguiled man into eating of the forbidden fruit, and since the fall, Satan has beguiled the creature into staying away from the Tree of Life. This great and dividing line of the spiritual against the ungodly or obedient versus the disobedient is found right throughout Scripture, and is there to bring glory to God through His people who are to burn as a bright and eternal light amidst such horrible and Satanic darkness, "And

---

[41] A.W. Pink, ibid., p. 15.

the Lord said, Simon, Simon, behold, Satan hath desired to have you, that he may sift you as wheat" (Luke 22:31).

It is only once we have an understanding of Satan's lesser and physical control that we can appreciate the infinitely greater and salvation of Christ, "For by grace ye are saved through faith; and not of yourselves: it is the gift of God" (Ephesians 2:8). All the glory is in our glorious head, of whom His chosen stand as an utterly unworthy, yet redeemed, body. The covenant of Grace, thereby, stands as the greatest link throughout the entire Bible, and the church is the result and substance, whereby, both Jewish and Gentile believers alike are justified by faith as the true "children of Abraham" (Galatians 3:7). Yet to gain a greater appreciation of the origins of such Grace, we shall now consider the fall in greater detail.

CHAPTER 4

A PROMISE OF GRACE

Our Lord determines His true seed as those born of faith in his promise of Grace against which Satan's judgment is fully pronounced in Genesis 3:15. Known as the Protoevangelium, this is the first Gospel sermon ever preached for no sooner was the great wound of sin inflicted than the remedy of Grace was revealed, and without this seed shall no creature avoid sin, death, hell and everlasting damnation. In the midst of cursing the serpent, there is a promise of the will of God's decree immediately coming to pass in the seed of the women, by which our first parents are surely comforted and understood by it that "the vengeance due to the serpent would be the guarantee of mercy to themselves. Perhaps, however, by thus obliquely giving the promise, the Lord meant to say: -

> 'Not for your sakes do I this, O fallen man and woman, nor for the sake of your descendants; but for My own Name and honour's sake, that it be not profaned and blasphemed amongst the fallen spirits.'" [42]

---

[42] C.H Spurgeon, *Christ the Conqueror of Satan,* From The Metropolitan Tabernacle Pulpit, Vol. 22, No. 1326, November 26, 1876.

Our Lord's prayer reinforces this promise of redemption as preordained from eternity passed, "that they may behold my glory, which thou hast given me: for thou lovedst me before the foundation of the world" (John 17:24). These names of life are determined by the will of God's immutable decree, and despite the wiles of Satan, none can be removed, "thy people shall be delivered, every one that shall be found written in the book" (Daniel 12:1). Christ as infallible is the very seed by which all the promises of redemption are made and are complete, "According as he hath chosen us in him before the foundation of the world, that we should be holy and without blame before him in love" (Ephesians 1:4).

The general revelation of God is prior to His special revelation in point of time. "It does not come to man in the form of verbal communications, but in the facts, the forces, and the laws of nature, in the constitution and operation of the human mind, and in the facts and experience of history. In addition to the revelation of God in nature, we have His special revelation, which is embodied in scripture...This special revelation became necessary through the entrance of sin into the world." [43]

Faith, however, is not naturally inherent within man and is a spiritual Grace. It is both an obedient response to, and assurance of, God's special revelation, by which this assurance comprehends a faithful trust of the remission of sins for Christ's blood sake. "For it was impossible that thy conscience should look for anything at God's hand, except it first be assured that God is merciful to thee for Christ's sake." [44]

Perfect spiritual liberty within this promise of Grace is not possible on earth whilst our flesh does hinder, betray and so easily beset with sin. The term flesh essentially refers to the part of us that is alienated from God and does not like to be told what to

---

[43] Louis Berkhof, ibid., pp. 11-12.
[44] Martin Luther, *Commentary on Galatians*, Kregel Classics, 1979, p. 36.

do. It is the obstinate, unruly and rebellious side to our inner self which must be brought into subjection, "therefore brethren, we are debtors, not to the flesh, to live after the flesh" (Romans 8:12).

The spirit of a believer is the part of us that is open to God, is drawn to Him and is assisted by God's Spirit in desiring to put on the new man "which after God is created in righteousness and true holiness" (Ephesians 4:24). Satan will often tempt and buffet the flesh to draw a believer aside, for although we have the blessed sweetness of communion and prayer through God's Spirit as the first fruits of glory, we are significantly constrained and bound to earth, groaning says the Apostle Paul, awaiting that final deliverance, "from the bondage of corruption into the glorious liberty of the children of God" (Romans 8:21-22).

Grace itself, therefore, is favor shown where there is positive demerit shown in the one receiving it and is the antithesis of justice, for justice itself shows no pity and knows no mercy. "Divine grace is magnified only after the sin which is to be forgiven has first been recognized and acknowledged as exceeding great." [45] The Gospel replaces fallen Adam as our federal to that of Christ, for through Him is the incredible justice of God satisfied by His sinless obedience to fully uphold the covenant of works, "But where sin abounded, grace did much more abound" (Romans 5:20).

Grace is not exercised at the expense of divine justice either for the curse that fell on Adam and his posterity remains since the fall. "Against such a curse of the law does the Gospel now bless all the world, inasmuch as it crieth openly unto all that acknowledge their sins and repent." [46] The true character of God is also seen through this eternal promise as a holy, merciful, loving, kind and forgiving heavenly father, who is giving gifts to the Son. We as His elect are His bride: -

---

[45] Martin Luther, *Commentary on Romans*, ibid., p. 69.

[46] William Tyndale, *Selected Works*, Focus Christian Ministries Trust, 1986, p. 111.

"even as Christ also loved the church, and gave
himself for it" (Ephesians 5:25).

God, however, is not bound to give an account of His actions
to the creature for He has total liberty to save some and not others.
His justice is neither impeached or blemished for, "Hath not
potter power over the clay, of the same lump to make one vessel
unto honour another unto dishonour" (Romans 9:21). Nor is
there any unrighteousness in God for permitting some vessels for
destruction and others to be saved through His sovereign mercy
for God is glorified in two ways: -

Firstly, God shows forth His power in judgment by enduring
"with much longsuffering the vessels of wrath fitted to destruction"
(9:22). He is longsuffering in abiding with the sin and wickedness
of man because those in disobedience and rebellion are meet
for His wrath and their coming judgment. Antagonism to the
witnessing church and the persecution of Christians will also meet
His everlasting wrath and seal their judgment.

Secondly, He makes "known the riches of his glory on the
vessels of mercy, which he had afore appointed unto glory"
(Romans 9:23). These are His own people, who, as lively organs
of praise, walk in obedience and exalt His divine blessing and
providence throughout all generations.

But we must go back to the start of Genesis 3 to gain a greater
appreciation of the context and shine of this promise. "Now the
serpent was more subtle than any beast of the which the Lord
God had made. And he said unto the women, Yea hath God said,
Ye shall not eat of every tree of the garden" (Genesis 3:1,). John
Calvin says, "The innate subtlety of the serpent did not prevent
Satan from making use of the animal for the purpose of effecting
the destruction of man." [47] For it was Satan's design and oversee
that did lead to the forbidden fruit being taken and consumed by

---

[47] John Calvin, ibid., vol. 1, p. 140.

both Adam and Eve against the specific command of our Lord not to: - "she took of the fruit thereof, and did eat, and gave also unto husband with her; and he did eat" (Genesis 3:5).

PENAL SANCTION: -

God made a covenant of works with Adam not to eat of the Tree of the Knowledge of Good and Evil for which Adam in his pre-fallen and innocent state was put on righteous probation in order for him to sustain his blessed and eternal life. It was a test of Adam's loyalty and subjection to his Creator to prove just how sacred Adam held God's will in obedience. Before Eve was created, God spoke to Adam, as the representative head of mankind, who was able to fully comprehend and understand God's command made to him, "But of the tree of the knowledge of good and evil, thou shalt not eat of it: for in the day that thou eatest thereof thou shalt surely die" (Genesis 2:17).

Adam and Eve were not only rational and moral creatures, but our first parents had power and freedom to uphold their integrity to defend themselves by rejecting the temptation with abhorrence. "This is evident from the clearly revealed fact that they were under an indispensable obligation to yield perfect obedience unto God, and liable to deserved punishment for the least defect thereof." [48]

The Tree of Knowledge of Good and Evil was a symbol of the law by which Adam's violation failed God's test of obedience and bore the contamination of original sin into this world. God's just judgment and punishment for such corruption and disobedience is in perfect accord with His authority and justice and the immediate penal sanction administered immediately imputes both corporeal death in the body and spiritual death in the soul to all of mankind.

The serpent was not privy to the information that God had

---

[48] A. W Pink, *The Doctrine of Human Depravity*, ibid., p. 7.

given Adam, yet he did for his part firstly instill doubt into the mind of Eve, and secondly undermine the penalty of sin which infiltrates the first heresy into world by offering a greater happiness through disobedience, "And Adam was not deceived, but the woman being deceived was in the transgression" (1 Timothy 2:14). The covenant, however, was not broken when Eve ate of the forbidden fruit but, rather, when she gave it to Adam "and he did eat" (Genesis 3:6).

In a single act of disobedience, the earth is cursed and the creature is forever ruined by original sin, "cursed is the ground for thy sake" (Genesis 3:17). Servitude and hard bondage will now follow and, for the first time, death is now certain, which beforehand, was not present. Satan, in effect, has taken dominion of earth over man.

So this covenant of works, or covenant of obedience, did not last for very long for God foreknew that man would stumble and fall at the upholding of this one command for which God justly holds man ultimately accountable for his actions and deeds. A great plight now emerges of the creature, who, as caught amidst such a significant force of darkness (death), is still surrounded by so glorious and eternal light to which he can never physically reach or attain by his own merit or device for his mutable will is impotent in reaching to God as it is enslaved to a fallen and corrupt nature.

Only the promise of sovereign mercy through the covenant of redemption made in agreement between God the Father and God the Son can restore this plight, "But when the fullness of the time was come, God sent forth his Son, made of a woman, made under the law" (Galatians 4:4). Christ is, thereby, the propitiation for our sins: –

> "For he hath made him to be sin for us, who knew
> no sin; that we might be made the righteousness
> of God in him" (2 Corinthians 5:21).

In redeeming our situation over death, our Savior perfectly satisfied the commands of the law as required by the Father saying, "Father, if thou be willing, remove this cup from me: nevertheless, not my will, but thine, be done" (Luke 22:42). He destroyed Satan's power of death at Calvary when our heavenly Father placed on Him the eternal weight of our deserved wrath and punishment for sin.

He willingly endured the tyranny of the law and tasted our death "to be made like unto his brethren, that he might become a merciful and faithful high priest in all things pertaining to God" (Hebrews 2:17). Moreover, He "suffered being tempted" (Hebrews 2:18) just like we are in order that He may be approachable by His brethren. He never succumbed to temptation but upheld perfect and righteous obedience to God's law to truly become our human representative and federal head.

Yet during His incarnation and before His exaltation, He lived as a man in soul and body and as such was actively subject to the law of God just like the rest of mankind. His active engagement of all ceremonial obligation and civic functions of the law, whilst also upholding all precepts of the moral law, satisfied the legal requirements of both, "And being found in fashion as a man, he humbled himself, and became obedient unto death, even the death of the cross" (Philippians 2:8).

All symbols of ancient sacrifice, rites and ceremony are done thus away, for true worshippers "must worship him in spirit and in truth" (John 4:24) and His example of upholding the moral law confirms the perpetual validity of the law of the living God. So as our Savior was in the world, so we ought to be: -

"but thou shalt follow me" (John 13:36).

His obedience was also passive, "For what the law could not do, in that it was weak through the flesh, God sending his own Son in the likeness of sinful flesh, and for sin, condemned sin in the flesh" (Romans 8:3). In His human nature, the incarnate Lord voluntarily suffered and was subjugated to human weakness and frailties of the flesh in humiliation for His people that eventually led to the Cross. He is thus the sinner's legal substitute as God the Father placed upon Him our deserved punishment and chastisement in order that we might be saved from wrath through Him.

SEED OF THE WOMEN: -

From Genesis 3:15, the Old Testament and New Testament are, therefore, one and the same substance for Christ is the seed of the women which represents the new covenant. What transpires between the Old and the New Testament is not different for it is one and the same God and His everlasting covenant of Grace throughout both: –

> "Of which salvation the prophets have enquired and searched diligently, who prophesied of the grace that should come unto you...when it testified beforehand the sufferings of Christ, and the glory that should follow" (1 Peter 1:10-11).

Eternal redemption was ordained through the context of the fall for God's command relating to the rule of the knowledge of good and evil that was broken by Adam bore original sin and the consequence of death. The promised decree of restoration as determined from eternity past is unalterable because His knowledge is perfect, and He sees all things in one entire prospect before Him, "My counsel shall stand, and I will do all my pleasure" (Isaiah 46:10). God's faithfulness is unchanging, and His sovereign decree as known within Himself, and formed by Him, is also everlasting and immutable, yet are known through the redemption of His elect.

These counsels shall stand, or be accomplished, by Him who is all wise, all knowing, unchangeable and faithful and true. Everything is perfectly ordained to secure eternal life for His bride, "I delight to do thy will, O my God: yea thy law is within my heart" (Psalm 40:8). His infallible and unchanging will is also effected towards the bride of His elect by means of all-sufficient and irresistible Grace, and nothing can be hindered: -

"For who hath resisted his will" (Romans 9:19).

"The purpose of God, and immutability of his counsel, Heb 6:16. have their certainty and firmness from eternity, and do not depend on the variable lubricity of mortal men, which we must need grant, unless we intend to set up impotency against omnipotency, and arm the clay against the potter." [49]

The righteous purpose of God is also declared and written upon the heart and conscience of man (Romans 2:15), yet children of the elect are not loved for any good works, just as evil works are not the cause of the decree of rejection. The Apostle Paul reinforces this, "For the children being not yet born, neither having done any good or evil, that the purpose of God according to election might stand, not of works, but of him that calleth" (Romans 9:11). God is ever faithful and His eternal decree is immutable in redeeming His elect.

MAN IS LOST: -

But let us consider divine providence further and ask why our marvelous a Creator did allow such ruin and misery to become the creature? Had the promise of life been given to Adam immediately after he was first created, for example, then man would not die, for if sin did enter as was the case by Satan's deceit, or if Adam had

---

[49] The Works of John Owen, Vol. 5, ibid., p .64

have fallen on his own accord, then there is already a promise of life. Knowing also that changeableness and mutability are both defining characteristics of the creature, would this promise of redemption really mean much to a creature that had life in the soul anyway, as death could not possibly enter? Would he really get down on his knees and thank the Lord for His mercy and clemency were there no such serious jeopardy of death? Moreover, "his faith would be a presumption and he would be unthankful to God and merciless unto his neighbour." [50]

God, who did create us, knows that for mankind to really appreciate what it means to be alive, he must first taste the horrible labors, bondage, sweat, loss, and tumult associated with death. Against such pain, suffering, famine, war, corruption, toil, failure, pestilence, pride, deceit, cunning, jealousy, and vanity of vanities, man is completely crushed and beaten with many stripes.

God's providential design of salvation through the fall also grants believers a far greater understanding of our Creator than without such a bleak outlook. Angels cannot appreciate this love as much as saved sinners do, "which things the angels desire to look into" (1 Peter 1:12). And because the second person of the Trinity, the Godman has assumed human flesh forever, we are more intimately connected with him in ways that angels cannot.

Yet, what must natural man do, and where, if any, can he turn as his greatest disposition is firmly before him now for he is facing death, and is in the midst of death in that he cannot uphold the mandates of God's will by any merit of his own? But death, in its eternal and ruinous force field, offers no answer and nor can it be expected to, for it was not designed for any conclusive end, but to rupture and condemn man over and over again in a never ending and vicious cycle.

What a horrible plight, for a sinner is not only spiritually dead in the soul, but is also walking with Satan, whether unwittingly

[50] William Tyndale, ibid., p. 87.

or otherwise, "according to the course of this world" (Ephesians 2:2). Carnal man's enmity against God would draw deserved condemnation unless the Spirit graciously awakened a sinner to God's promise of redemption to restore life. It is also the gift of the Spirit that illuminates our spiritual need seeking after the Lord: -

> "for who maketh thee to differ? and what hast
> thou that didst not receive" (1 Corinthians 4:7).

REGENERATION: -

God's gracious call towards repentance is, therefore, unmistakable, "incline your ear, and come unto me: hear, and your soul shall live" (Isaiah 55:3). How closely does the creature now abide in the Spirit in asking the Lord for forgiveness?

It is an amazing gift and joy to see the Spirit's regenerating work in implanting new life into the soul, whereby, God slowly draws and awakens a sinner to eternal realities and considerations: -

> "No man can come unto me, except the Father
> which hath sent me draw him" (John 6:44).

Conversion begins with an act of God. "Those who are drawn are taught by God, and their wills made open to believe. The word draw itself does not indicate that the sinner is merely attracted or invited to come to Christ. The word in the original Greek means to draw effectively. The word also indicates the listless nature of the thing that needs to be drawn." [51]

A sinner is spiritually awakened and convicted after the effectual call for he now sees the darkness and heinous nature of sin and his lost predicament before a holy and righteous God. Repentance and (saving) faith now follows which is the true heart

---

[51] Peter Masters, *Physicians of Souls,* Wakeman Trust, 2002, pp. 39-40.

of the Gospel in illuminating men to "repentance toward God and faith our Lord Jesus Christ" (Acts 20:21). A believer at this point will see firmly and cling hold of the finished work of Christ which does impart new life: -

> "Being born again, not of corruptible seed but of incorruptible, by the word of God" (1 Peter 1:23).

It cannot be stressed just how much Satan is intently watching and observing a sinner drawn by Grace for he does not want any of his captives to leave his fold of darkness. Satan is a spirit, and as the Holy Spirit does communicate and illuminate our minds through our own spirit, so will Satan try to tempt and throw all manner of doubts into our minds as to our standing in the faith. He wants to undermine the special peace and joy in believing, but Christ's protective hand is always there to comfort, "Peace I leave you, my peace I give unto you…let not your heart be troubled, neither be afraid" (John 14:27).

Faith, therefore, is not the cause of the new spiritual birth, but the consequence of it for the blessed work of the Spirit precedes our believing and forgiveness, "Mercy and truth are met together; righteousness and peace have kissed each other" (Psalm 85:10). Justification declares a believer's right to everlasting life and also identifies our existence in Christ, whereby, the gracious Spirit imparts peace and blessed assurance to begin to walk in newness of life away from sin.

Believers are eternally adopted and ratified by His shed blood as the mediator between God the Father and lost mankind, all of which is solemnly authenticated and sealed "by that holy spirit of promise" (Ephesians 2:13). This holy certification into the body of Christ is for and by His sovereign purpose and design that we may suffer afflictions with Christ in bearing witness to His truth.

For a sinner to come to the actual point of conversion can take quite a period of time but it is essential in our walk of faith to know that believers are set apart at conversion. It is the first steps in a holy consecration to come into His likeness, "Ye shall be Holy, for I am Holy" (Leviticus 11:44).

God looks upon the intent of the heart and will never turn away a genuine and penitent heart so humbled before Him. It is a touching pleasure for God to see such appeal for His eternal pardon and clemency for it places a total dependence upon Him who imparts this through Grace. Furthermore, the Lord's mercy is longsuffering and patient in drawing sinners to Himself, "full of compassion; slow to anger, and of great mercy" (Psalm 145:8). Yet this humility must be directed solely towards Him: –

"he will fill the desire of them that fear him: he will also hear their cry, and will save them" (Psalm 145:19).

Sincerity itself, however, is not an assurance of true conversion, for many like Jehovah's witnesses for example, who despite showing unquestionable diligence, have been falsely led astray and are ultimately misguided in the belief of salvation by works. Only Christ can secure reconciliation between God and His creation, between heaven and earth: -

"in whom we have redemption through his blood" (Ephesians. 1:7).

Victory is assured for "He who overcometh, the same shall be clothed in white raiment; and I will not blot out his name out of the book of life, and I will confess his name before my Father, and before his angels" (Revelation 3:5).

Yet in following our Savior, the context of overcoming for believers is made "perfect through sufferings" (Hebrews 2:10) for "both he that sanctifieth and they who are sanctified are all one: for which cause he is not ashamed to call them brethren" (Hebrews

2:11). It is, thereby, a refining process of the heart for which the holy and righteous character of Christ is imparted gradually in life and totally at death when all believers are translated into eternity.

We have thus considered the promise of Grace through the backdrop of the fall to our Lord's incarnation and living a perfect life of obedience to fulfill the law. Yet the exact nature and terms of the agreement between God the Father and God the Son in the covenant of redemption that enacts the covenant of Grace through His elect to mankind are what we shall next consider in greater detail.

CHAPTER 5

COVENANT OF REDEMPTION

God's eternal plan of redemption throughout history addresses the fundamental question of how might sinful man, which is every human creature born since Adam, attain everlasting Life (salvation) through the forgiveness of sin. How fallen and sinful mankind ruined by the fall can come back to God is prescribed very clearly throughout Scripture, as God says to Moses at the burning bush, "And he said, Draw not nigh hither: put off thy shoes from off thy feet, for the place whereon thou standest is holy ground" (Exodus 3:5).

A sinner cannot, therefore, nonchalantly approach God, for there are certain requirements and patterns that must be followed, including a spirit of prayer that fosters an enormous reverence and humility as to His absolute majesty and holiness through His Word.

God's faithfulness sovereign purpose for salvation cannot be changed either for the will of His eternal decree concerning redemption is immutable. A covenant, therefore, has two sides in that firstly it is a sure and stable promise, ordinance and precept (or rule) from God, "And he said, Behold, I make a covenant: before all thy people I will do marvels, such as have not been done in all the earth, nor in any nation: and all the people among which thou art shall see the work of the Lord: for it is a terrible thing that I will do with thee" (Exodus 34:10).

The nation, or theocracy, of Israel, was promised and fulfilled by the immediate directive of God, for which Moses was given laws to extend and develop this nation through a common administration, and a code of law that gives the nation its constitution and structure, without which it cannot survive. Yet, the general refusal of ethnic Israel to accept and embrace the many privileges extended to them by God serves as a great and "terrible" warning to wider Gentile nations in this Gospel age. As a type of the church, national Israel attests to the fact that when one is faithful to God, He blesses; when one is unfaithful, He disciplines; and when one repents, God forgives and begins to bless once again.

Divine providence and blessing befell the nation of Israel for it was through the physical bloodline and lineage of the Jews that the Messiah was born. This is seen in the genealogy of Christ in both Matthew 1:1-16 which traces His lineage from Solomon to Joseph as the legal Son, and in Luke 3:23-38 where Christ's lineage is traced from David's son Nathan to Mary as the blood Son. David, as a type of Christ, reigned over the house of Israel from his throne in Jerusalem, by which promised Messiah was born through from David's physical seed as a Jew, "He shall be great, and shall be called the Son of the Highest: and the Lord God shall give unto him the throne of his father David" (Luke 1:32).

This promise is also spiritually fulfilled for the Messiah has established an everlasting Kingdom from which He reigns from His throne above as high priest and King to govern the affairs of His people, "And in that day there shall be a root of Jesse, which shall stand for an ensign of the people; to it shall the Gentiles seek: and his rest shall be glorious," (Isaiah 11:10). Such a throne also denotes the King's absolute power and authority to fulfil such a promise: -

> "If thy children will keep my covenant and my
> testimony that I shall teach them, their children

shall also sit upon thy throne for evermore"
(Psalms 132:12).

As circumcision was stipulated upon Abraham and his
descendants as a picture of obedience, so too are the particular
sons of David instructed to remain faithful to God and His laws
or face the consequences. In a typical sense, "this not only affirms
the unconditional right of David's sons to the throne but also
emphasized that each son of David had to attend to his duties as the
ruler of Israel for only those who were faithful to the covenant could
expect to participate in the blessings promised to David's house." [52]

Spiritually, however, such conditions were not fulfilled by
successive leaders of natural and ethnic Israel. They stood at
variance, as an offense, to God through disobedience, whose
circumcision was outward, of the flesh, and not of the heart, "For
they would not walk in his ways, neither were they obedient unto
his law" (Isaiah 42:24).

AGREEMENT: -

The second and more regular use for a covenant in Scripture is,
therefore, a mutual agreement or promise between two parties
with respect to something. Three examples that highlight specific
agreements, promises or a pact between various parties are: -

a. Genesis 14:13 we see the context as allies between
    Abraham, Mamre, Eshcol and Ener who form a
    confederacy to rescue Lot.
b. In Genesis 26:18-19 Isaac and Abimelech the king of the
    Philistines create an oath or covenant of peace together at
    Beersheeba.

---

[52] Dr. Richard Pratt, *God of Covenant,* Reformed Perspectives Magazine,
Volume 10, Number 5, January 27 to February 2, 2008.

c.   1 Samuel 18:3 we see a covenant between Jonathan and David, "because he loved him as his own soul."

As foreordained before the foundation of the world, and the oldest of all covenants, the covenant of redemption, is an agreement between God the Father and God the Son that determines the way that mankind can obtain consummate, eternal blessedness and happiness, for God "is a rewarder of them that diligently seek him" (Hebrews 11:6). This reward and diligence, however, is entwined with a threat of eternal destruction in which the contender for happiness (man) will be punished in that way without such an agreement of mercy and pardon from God. The covenant stands as righteous obedience to the Lord by faith in the promises of God: -

> "By whom we have received grace and apostleship,
> for obedience to the faith among all nations, for
> his name" (Romans 1:5).

The law, as an expression of God's character, is perfectly compatible with God's love, for despite sin being a breach of God's law, His reconciling love mercifully restores life and everlasting peace: -

> "because the love of God is shed abroad in our
> hearts by the Holy Ghost which is given unto us"
> (Romans 5:5).

It cuts and strikes a death blow for the unregenerate, however, for the word covenant in the Hebrew literally means to cut. God made a covenant with Abraham who is instructed to present an animal that would be cut in two before laying each piece one against another. God then seals the agreement between both parties, "And it came to pass, that, when the sun went down, and it was dark, behold a smoking furnace, and a burning lamp that passed between those pieces" (Genesis 15:17).

The Lord passed through the midst of the carnage of those pieces in the form of a "smoking furnace, and a burning lamp" (Genesis 15:17), taking the consequence of the curse upon Himself. Thus does bloodletting and slaying have a very real application for the remission of sin, for as both redeemer and head of the elect, the Son presents Himself as surety on their behalf: -

> "By so much was Jesus made a surety of a better testament" (Hebrews 7:22).

God's universal ordinance and precepts are both immutable for they reveal the mandate of His known will, which is founded upon the abiding and enduring testament of God. So certain is this testament that there would be no succession of day and night if God's redemptive purpose did not stand as accomplished towards His spiritual seed, or the body of His elect, which is the antitype and fulfillment of David, "If my covenant be not with day and night, and if I have not appointed the ordinances of heaven and earth; then will I cast away the seed of Jacob and David my servant" (Jeremiah 33:25-26).

ORDINATION: -

The law of nature was violated in Adam through his transgression of the rule of the knowledge of good and evil. Immediately did guilt, corruption and inadequacy before God arise as man's previously infallible nature was violated, "I heard thy voice in the garden, and I was afraid, because I was naked; and I hid myself" (Genesis 3:10). Although violated, mortal man's conscience, is still alive after the fall, but inwardly, the finite creature must now contend with all manner of sinful desires and evil lusts which are opposed to good works.

God's ordination, or the doctrine of concurrence, implies that man, despite all of his faculties, cannot act independently from God, for the creature can only act by a power given unto them which is also distinct from them, "For in him we live, and move, and have our being...For we are also his offspring" (Acts 17:28). "His immutability and impeccability (non-liability to sin) are qualities that essentially distinguish the Creator from the creature - the angels possess neither as the fall of at least one third of their number (Rev. 12) demonstrated." [53]

God is the author and first cause for He acts and everything else is subsequent to His action. Furthermore, nothing acts upon God for the human will cannot act autonomously outside of God's influence and a secondary cause cannot act unless it is first acted upon. God must firstly act in order for the creature to act accordingly, "And shall not God avenge his own elect, which cry day and night unto him, though he bear long with them" (Luke 18:7).

As our covenant head, His people are called out of ruin solely by God's promise of Grace for just as Adam's sin is imputed to all, so does Christ's death impute righteousness to all who would believe on Him by faith: -

> "For as by one man's disobedience many were made sinners, so by the obedience of one shall many be made righteous" (Romans 5:19).

The fall, however, does not abrogate the duty to keep the law for mankind is under the covenant of works and, therefore, anybody who does not uphold perfect obedience will face a just and eternal death. In this sense, the law's divine design will ever have an abiding effect and it will always accomplish the purpose for which it was given for man's inability to obey does not negate

---

[53] A. W Pink, *The Doctrine of Human Depravity*, ibid., p. 7.

his responsibility to obey, "Because the law worketh wrath: for where no law is, there is no transgression" (Romans 4:15).

As man's sin is the cause of his inability, God cannot accommodate the creatures' altered capacities and inclinations for the righteousness required of the covenant of works is rooted in His immutable nature. The law perpetually remains valid because it mirrors God's divine and everlasting glory:-

> "Every good gift and every perfect gift is from above, and cometh down from the Father of lights, with whom is no variableness, neither shadow of turning" (James 1:17).

Before God, man cannot fulfill anything in his natural and carnal state and it is God who has seen fit to annex the promise of life to obedience to His law. This is a double negative for not only can no creature render and uphold such strict and necessary obedience, but the law also denounces death as the penalty for transgression, "For the wages of sin is death" (Romans 6:24). God's promise of redemption is very much the positive and good news in cleaving to Christ by faith to become a new creature through His finished work at Calvary in perfectly fulfilling all moral requirements of the law.

REDEMPTION: -

Believers are, therefore, unconditionally saved from condemnation from the curse of the law only because Christ our federal head has fulfilled all manner of obedience in offering Himself as a righteous and vicarious sacrifice. Conversely, those outside of Grace are accursed as they are subject to fulfill the entirety of the law by which no creature can bear in seeking for justification by their own works and are literally cut off from such mercy in not turning to, and rejecting, Christ, "For I testify again to every man that is circumcised, that he is a debtor to do the whole law" (Galatians 5:3).

As God is the initiator, man is bound to accept the covenant as required by the law for which he cannot reject or attempt to re-negotiate the precepts in any way as this represents who we are to be if we are to abide and reflect His holy and righteous will. It is God's perfect redemption plan by which we have certain hope and "not to desire the promises is to refuse the goodness of God." [54]

> "And I appoint unto you a kingdom, as my Father
> hath appointed unto me" (Luke 22:29).

It is a primary doctrine, as either asserted or assumed throughout the Scripture, that we are under the law of God as binding upon all classes of men, whether they enjoy a divine revelation or not. "Everything which God has revealed as a rule of duty enters into the constitution of the law, which binds those to whom that revelation is given and by which they are to be ultimately judged. Those who have not received any external revelation of the divine will are a law unto themselves. The knowledge of right and wrong, written upon their hearts, is of the nature of a divine law, having its authority and sanction, and by it the heathen are to be judged in the last day." [55]

The unrighteous cannot save himself for only God can restore unto His people true liberty, and is why Grace abounds throughout the Old Testament as well by faith, "I, even I, am the Lord; and beside me there is no saviour" (Isaiah 43:11). The covenant of redemption demands satisfaction of an infinite, perfect and unblemished expiatory sacrifice from a righteous man in order to fulfill that which was violated and broken in the

[54] Matthew McMahan, *Covenant Theology Series*, Still Water Revival Books, https://www.sermonaudio.com/sermons.asp?keyword=covenant+theology+series, Part 1, 01/01/2002.

[55] Charles Hodge, ibid., p. 2.

covenant of works by the creature at the fall and in removing the guilt that did originate thereby.

Biblically there has to be a legal purity for God the Father to firstly accept this sacrifice and secondly, the sacrifice must completely satisfy the divine justice demanded by the law, "For there is one God and one mediator between God and men, the man Christ Jesus" (1 Timothy 2:5). This propitiation and expiation for the sin of the elect is only accepted through the shed blood of Christ and His all-sufficient sacrifice.

A testator comes on behalf of others to do something, which means that Christ is Lord of His life in being able to lay down His life for others and becoming our surety, "No man taketh it from me, but I lay it down of myself. I have power to lay it down and I have power to take it again. This commandment have I received of my Father" (John 10:18). "What He did in dying, He was able to do," [56] and the matchless Love of God is fully manifest through Christ in offering Himself as a sacrifice on behalf of His people.

Regenerating the souls of His people for everlasting life glorifies God in the highest for only God can raise man back to its proper state and into the true image of God from its fallen and depraved condition, "Who hath saved us, and called us with an holy calling, not according to our works, but according to his own purpose and grace, which was given us in Christ Jesus before the world began" (2 Timothy 1:9).

REWARD AND OBEDIENCE: -

Our Savior's glory was veiled in human flesh during His during His earthly ministry, "And now, O Father, glorify thou me with thine own self with the glory which I had with thee before the world was" (John 17:5). He rightfully longed to be exalted but it was not until after His resurrection that He had a new glorified

---

[56] Matthew McMahon, ibid., part 14, 05/12/2006.

body and is given a name above all names because as our human representative or Godman. He finished what He came to do in fulfilling the covenant of works: -

> "And for their sakes I sanctify myself, that they also might be sanctified through the truth" (John 17:19).

Thus are His elect liberated from the yoke and tyranny the law for He has more dominion, authority and power than any, for He is "Far above all principality, and power, and might, and dominion, and every name that is named, not only in this world, but also in that which is to come" (Ephesians 1:21). In fulfilling all manner of righteous obedience according to the flesh, He "hath put all things under his feet, and gave him to be the head over all things to the church" (Ephesians 1:22).

Our Lord, once risen, confirms His exaltation, "And Jesus came and spake unto them, saying, "All power is given unto me in heaven and in earth" (Matthew 28:18). He is the sustainer of the church which is abundantly rewarded in the Spirit, "Blessed be the Lord, who daily loadeth us with benefits, even the God of our salvation" (Psalm 68:19). His people are thus anointed in the highest, "Thou lovest righteousness, and hatest wickedness: therefore God, thy God, hath anointed thee with oil of gladness above thy fellows" (Psalm.45:7).

As co-eternal within the Godhead Trinity from eternity past, the Holy Spirit was also present in Old Testament times, in striving and comforting men towards the promise of redemption. This is evidenced by the regeneration of Joshua the high priest, "Take away the filthy garments from him...Behold, I have caused thine iniquity to pass from thee, and I will clothe thee with a change of raiment" (Zechariah 3:4).

The same Spirit that led Isaiah during his ministry, "The Spirit of the Lord God is upon me; because the Lord hath anointed me to preach good tidings unto the meek; he hath sent me to bind up the broken hearted, to proclaim liberty to the captives, and the opening of the prison to them that are bound" (Isaiah 63:1), also molded and guided Samuel in Grace, "And Samuel grew, and the Lord was with him and did not let none of his words fall to the ground" (1 Samuel 3:19). Likewise, "The Spirit of the Lord came upon Saul" (1 Samuel 11:6) after he was anointed as the first king of Israel, and despite acting foolishly with the Philistines in not keeping the commandments of the Lord (1 Samuel 13:13), and his second sin at Gilgal in rejecting the Word of the Lord (1 Samuel 15:23), God did direct the affairs of Israel through him in providing a king.

During Old Testament times, however, the Spirit did not permanently reside or indwell a believer like today, for a more abundant effusion of the Spirit was not imparted until our Savior was thus exalted. Christ had to leave heaven to send the Spirit by His full power and authority upon His return in order to gather His people back: –

> "Wherefore he saith, When he ascended up on high, he led captivity captive, and gave gifts unto men" (Ephesians 4:8).

He gives gifts to the church in this present Gentile and Gospel age in a far greater and extensive capacity as a risen actual Lord and Savior, for the covenant of Grace becomes effectual when God's Spirit joins himself with the chariot of His Word: -

> "Therefore being by the right hand of God exalted, and having received of the Father the promise of the Holy Ghost, he hath shed forth this, which ye now see and hear" (Acts 2:33).

This obedience throughout His humiliation completely merits the reward as the highest and perfect fruition of God and all authority at the right hand of God, where His exaltation and reign are made complete: –

"Therefore will I divide him a portion with the great, and he shall divide the spoil with the strong" (Isaiah 53:12).

God must react to sin for God cannot deny Himself and, thereby, does His majesty and perfection justly propagate such condemnation and wrath against sin by the law. It is a manifestation of His holiness that He cannot be joined to a sinner without satisfaction, "Thou art of purer eyes than to behold evil, and canst not look on iniquity: wherefore lookest thou upon them that deal treacherously, and holdest thy tongue when the wicked devoureth the man that is more righteous than he?" (Habakkuk 1:13).

He cannot look upon sin and must make an account, "For thou art not a God that hath pleasure in wickedness: neither shall evil dwell with thee. The foolish shall not stand in thy sight: thou hatest all workers of iniquity. Thou shalt destroy them that speak leasing: the Lord will abhor the bloody and deceitful man" (Psalm 4:5-6).

God doesn't derive pleasure in the fall and destruction of the wicked or for His creation to continue on its wicked path to destruction but He is consoled by His perfect justice to punish sin, "And it shall come to pass, that as the Lord rejoiced over you to do you good, and to multiply you; so the Lord will rejoice over you to destroy you, and to bring you to nought" (Deuteronomy 28:63).

The Lord also says, "For I have no pleasure in the death of him that dieth...wherefore turn yourselves, and live ye" (Ezekiel 18:32). It is just and necessary to punish wickedness, for no matter how small sin is it is still infinitely horrendous and heinous to God and must be punished for an infinite duration that cannot be removed or satisfied without Christ's blood.

"The wicked have a never-dying worm, and the godly

a never-fading crown," [57] for God either sees the sin and its perpetrator as infinitely condemned or as infinitely covered by Christ's blood. There is no middle ground for sin stands eternally damned without Christ's blood, and a never-dying worm represents the conscience of an unbeliever. "An unjustified sinner also has a lifetime to compound the infinite debt of sin that is meet for eternal death and punishment." [58] Mercifully, however, God stays His hand of judgment in longsuffering love: -

> "The Lord is not slack concerning his promise, as some men count slackness; but is longsuffering to us-ward, not willing that any should perish, but that all should come to repentance" (2 Peter 3:9).

COVENANT OF GRACE: -

The new covenant of Grace, therefore, replaces the faulty covenant of works from Genesis 3:15. Works are faulty in that, firstly, the covenant was broken by Adam and, secondly, works extract a "ministration of death" (2 Corinthians 3:7) through condemnation from the Mosaic law. Through such curse, God progressively reveals more details of Grace, and how man may attain unto it, through the various covenants of the Old Testament until the manifestation of this promise fulfills all requirements of the law in the person of our Lord and lays upon Him our deserved punishment as sin-bearer for His people.

The covenant of Grace is, thereby, the vehicle by which God's blessing and privileges bear fruit in the salvation of His people and is the greatest link that emanates throughout the entire Scripture. Old Testament saints knew less of God's revelation than what we now know in New Testament times but it does not make us any

---

[57] Thomas Watson, ibid., p. 63.
[58] Matthew McMahon, ibid., part 7, 02/28/2006.

better than what they were because they still had faith in the same promise: -

> "These all died in faith, not having received the promises, but having seen them afar off, and were persuaded of them, and embraced them, and confessed that they were strangers and pilgrims on the earth" (Hebrews 11:13).

The covenant of redemption, however, is foundational in our understanding as to why the Son was sent for Christ is the very seed by which all the promises are made and are complete, "And this I say, that the covenant, that was confirmed before of God in Christ, the law, which was four hundred and thirty years after, cannot disannul, that it should make the promise of none effect" (Galatians 3:17). In the covenant of Grace, God makes an agreement with the elect, and, thereby, mankind, the conditions by which are met through what Christ has fulfilled in His agreement with the Father: -

> "Who verily was foreordained before the foundation of the world, but was manifest in these last times for you" (1 Peter 1:20).

The Son could not withdraw from this covenant as God's promises would have been nullified and come to nothing if our Lord did not do what He agreed. He was bound by the eternal will of His decree and sovereign purpose to do what He did at Calvary, "That by two immutable things, in which it was impossible for God to lie, we might have a strong consolation, who have fled for refuge to lay hold upon the hope set before us" (Hebrews 6:18).

It is impossible in the immutability of His oath and council to lie and it would have been a sin to break and not fulfill the covenant of redemption in His human nature. The very essence of Christianity in having our sins covered through the atoning death and imputed righteousness of Christ would be void, yet our Lord demonstrates that He is truly Messiah in fulfilling the covenant because He could not withdraw from the unconditional law of love: -

> "Greater love hath no man than this, that a man
> lay down his life for his friends" (John 15:13).

DIVINE COUNSEL: -

It is this intrinsic nature of the covenant of redemption that gives rise to the covenant of Grace for in bearing a human nature, Christ first receives power from the Father to fulfill the commands of the law on behalf of His people, "No man taketh it from me, but I lay it down of myself. I have power to lay it down, and I have power to take it again. This commandment have I received of my Father" (John 10:18). By this perfect obedience to fulfill this covenant, He is the overall anointed one of God and covenant head: -

> "Wherefore God also hath highly exalted him,
> and given him a name which is above every name"
> (Philippians 2:9).

Adam was under the same covenant of works by which all of mankind is bound but original sin is not propagated or imputed to Christ for our Lord was born not of natural conception but supernatural conception, "And the angel answered and said unto her, The Holy Ghost shall come upon thee, and the power of the Highest shall overshadow thee" (Luke 1:35). The miracle of the virgin birth meant that Messiah was preserved and immunised from original sin, by which such embryonic sanctification, that did propagate all the Graces and gifts required for His babyhood in being holy, harmless and undefiled and separate from sinners, did emanate not from Mary as God's chosen vessel to bear our Incarnate Lord into this world, but from the Spirit.

The inherent power and presence of the Spirit in maintaining our Lord's pattern for holiness and witness throughout His earthly ministry, preserved His body sinless, for as both utterly and fully man and utterly and fully God, one sin or tinge of disobedience would have nullified God's entire plan and purpose in redemption –

> "How much more shall the blood of Christ, who through the eternal Spirit, offered himself without spot to God, purge your conscience from dead works to serve the living God?" (Hebrews 9:14).

Thus is the blessed government of God's faithful and sovereign purpose to redeem firmly "upon his shoulder" (Isaiah 9:6). Our Lord's baptism also seals and authenticates the promise of redemption and counsel of peace between the Trinity, "And the Holy Ghost descended in a bodily shape like a dove upon him, and a voice came from heaven, which said, Thou art my beloved Son; in thee I am well pleased" (Luke 3:22). This symbolizes the seal of the Holy Spirit that follows all believers who are adopted as sons into the body of Christ, who is our covenant head: -

> "Nevertheless the foundation of God standeth sure, having this seal, 'The Lord knoweth them that are his" (2 Timothy 2:19).

THE LORD'S EARTHLY MINISTRY: -

In commencing His public ministry, our Lord undertook His particular office as Prophet, Priest, and King, and was given full gifts of the Spirit without measure (John 3:34) as seen by 3 distinct aspects: -

Firstly, as Christ was thrust by the Spirit into the wilderness to gain victory in His conflict over Satan to establish His Kingdom, so to does the Spirit thrust out His servants throughout all ages of Christian history into the wilderness of this world to overcome the evil one and share in His mighty victory in establishing the Kingdom of God in every corner of the earth. For as Christ received the Spirit without measure, so to do His people receive the ministry of the Spirit by the measure of Grace and faith given unto them to both walk in the steps of Savior and to keep in touch with His Spirit.

Secondly, He receives the Spirit particularly for His works of power, for in the finger of God, that is through the Spirit, does He cast out demons and perform miracles that authenticate His ministry. Blasphemy against the Spirit is such a serious sin because it is not only direct opposition to the Spirit but is direct opposition to the Lord Jesus who is not only the bearer of the Spirit but who in another sense is also the instrument of the Spirit in establishing the Kingdom of God. He was also endowed with the Spirit for His preaching and teaching ministry many of His hearers were arrested by the graciousness of His words: -

"Never man spake like this man" (John 7:46).

Thirdly, our Lord offered Himself as a divine sacrifice and atonement for sin which stands in complete opposition to the sacrifice of the Old Testament for the supreme sacrifice of Christ is offered in the power of the Spirit of God. It is a divinely appointed sacrifice in that the one who offered it was divinely enabled by Spirit. Moreover, sacrifice in Old Testament times was the blood of goats or of calves made on coals of fire on a man-made alter, whereas the sacrifice of Christ is made without spot or blemish upon the burning seal of the Savior, as inspired and "justified in the Spirit" (1 Timothy 3:16).

Great Puritan divine, John Owen, says that "here is the

epitome of what He is able to say, that the seal of His Father's house, His Father's glory, and His Father's people has consumed Him. It is the consuming agency of the power of the Spirit that enables the Lord to offer Himself as an all-atoning sacrifice." [59] Thus does holiness and humanity meet together in the lives of God's people.

Our Lord, thereby, delights to fulfill the will of the Father, "Then said he, Lo, I come to do thy will, O God," (Hebrews 10:9) and as our surety, He has purchased eternal clemency in complete and perfect satisfaction before God the Father in fulfilling all manner of righteousness demanded by the law. It is not a mere possibility but is certainly set in the decree of His immutable will and in the power of His oath, which represents the sure aspect of being saved, "for such an high priest became us, who is holy, harmless, undefiled, separate from sinners, and made higher than the heavens" (Hebrews 7:26).

God cannot forbear sin which means that the essential character and nature of God is perfectly satisfied in reconciling the Father's inherent goodness, holiness, and justice to the commands of the law.

This propitiation demonstrates the infinite value, righteousness and truth of Christ and His obedience and suffering in the flesh to fulfill the covenant of redemption and purchase everlasting life for His elect, who, thereby, possess the right to be sons and heirs to His salvation, "But as many as received him, to them gave he power to become sons of God" (John 1:12). Natural man simply cannot demand or affect anything in its previous unregenerate and innate carnal condition before conversion: -

---

[59] Sinclair B. Ferguson, *John Owen on the Holy Spirit*, https://www.sermonaudio.com/sermoninfo.asp?SID=112207111302, part 1, 22/11/2007.

"For you are brought with a price: therefore,
glorify God in your body, and in your spirit,
which are God's" (1 Corinthians 6:20).

Christ, therefore, takes upon His elect as in a marriage for we
"are members of his body, of his flesh and his bones" (Ephesians
5:30). It is a blessed and everlasting union into His body that
matches the real human body of flesh and bones that He bore in
purchasing our eternal redemption. And whilst the host of His
elect are eternally indebted to Him for such matchless obedience,
holiness, and submission, the Son is in no way indebted to the
Father, for He is co-equal with the Father from eternity and as
such, the command for justice is unified: -

"For I have not spoken of myself; but the Father
which sent me, he gave me a commandment, what
I should say, and what I should speak" (John
12:49).

The Father also prepared a body that the person of the Son
could inhabit before His death at Calvary and His subsequent
resurrection, "Wherefore when he cometh into the world, he saith,
Sacrifice and offering thou wouldest not, but a body hast thou
prepared me" (Hebrews 10:5).

Despite our Savior's willing suffering in both active and
passive obedience of the flesh in order to satisfy the justice of the
law, it was still God the Father who poured the terrible and eternal
weight of damnation upon Him in the short space of six hours
upon the Cross to appease our deserved wrath for sin: -

"Yet it pleased the Lord to bruise him; he hath
put him to grief: when thou shalt make his soul
an offering for sin, he shall see his seed, he shall

prolong his days, and the pleasure of the Lord shall prosper in his hand" (Isaiah 53:10).

But exactly who God's covenant people are in receiving such eternal blessing is something that we shall next examine for Satan has tried to divide God's people from both the Old and New Testament through the doctrinal error known as dispensationalism.

CHAPTER 6

GOD'S COVENANT PEOPLE

The true church has always endured persecution as evident very early in Genesis 4 with the account of Cain and Abel, for "Abel offered unto God a more excellent sacrifice than Cain" (Hebrews 11:4). Abel, in Godly and heartfelt obedience, offered a better sacrifice to God which grieved Cain to such an extent that he rose up in anger and murdered Abel. God looks upon the obedience of our heart, which is why Abel's offering was accepted over that of Cain, and God's sovereign will is still upheld for He quickly appoints "another seed instead of Abel whom Cain slew," (Genesis 4:25) for the Godly Line to continue through Seth.

The rudiments of this fallen world begin to quickly emerge, however, in the character of Lamech. There are two separate humanities, people and developing civilizations in Genesis 4 for which Lamech is the epitome of the ungodly, carnal, and unregenerate line. They represent souls which are not counted for eternal life and stand outside of Grace in living only for the here and now as boastful, humanistic and God forsaking. Lamech leads this great charge and is delusional with his cry, "if Cain shall be avenged sevenfold, truly Lamech seventy and seven" (Genesis 4:24). This boasts a god of his own making and equates to nothing more than a total dependence upon self and his own might and strength to prevail.

Compare now the development of the royal reed or Godly

line from Genesis 5, where Seth begets Enos and follows through to Enoch, who as a sign of his true faith, "was translated that he should not see death…for before his translation he had this testimony, that he pleased God" (Hebrews 11:5). This true line always holds council with God and walks with Him personally and for it is the central gravity of all believers to follow the Lord and nothing else. A sense of and service pervade all believers for we are separated to do what the Lord requires: -

"to do justly, and to love mercy, and to walk humbly with thy God" (Micah 6:8).

Sovereign Grace now follows to Noah, who "found grace in the eyes of the Lord," and, "walked with God" (Genesis 6:8-9). Noah, lived in a particularly evil time where the sin of man reached up unto heaven, as any Godly distinction was eroded through mixed marriages, "for the sons of God saw the daughters of men… and they took them wives" (Genesis 6:2). As a consequence of this compromise, God determined a great flood to arise "for forty days and forty nights" (Genesis 7:12) to cleanse the earth and destroy all wickedness. Yet amidst this darkness, Noah's faith did shine to build the ark, "Thus did Noah; according to all that God commanded him, so did he" (Genesis 6:22).

Noah and his family emerge from the ark and receive God's blessing to replenish the earth, whereby, God made a unilateral covenant with His creation to keep the arena of the earth functioning to accomplish His redemptive purpose to every generation: - "neither will I again smite any more everything living, as I have done" (Genesis 8:21).

Despite the wickedness upon earth crying out for destruction and vengeance every day, the Noahic covenant is unconditional with mankind for God limits His wrath to show forth His gracious and sovereign will. It is from the family of Noah that Gentile nations are also first prophesied to be included in the Godly Line,

"God shall enlarge Japheth, and he shall dwell in the tents of Shem" (Genesis 9:27). Thus does the Godly line now follow from Shem, down unto Nahor, who begat Terah, who begat Abram (Genesis 11:26).

ABRAM: -

As a picture of Grace, the first thing we see in Abraham (known as Abram at this stage meaning father of many) is that he, along with Sarai his wife and his nephew Lot, were called from idolatry by God to separation, "Get thee out of thy country, and from thy kindred...And I will make of thee a great nation, and I will bless thee, and make thy name great; and thou shalt be a blessing" (Genesis 12:1-2). "This calling to Abram is a great emblem to the calling of men by the Grace of God out of the world, and from among the men of it, and to renounce the things of it, and not to be conformed unto it...and to cleave to the Lord, and to follow Him withersoever He directs." [60]

This blessing of Abram is seen shortly after his call in being justified by faith in God's promise of redemption, "And he believed in the Lord, and he counted it to him for righteousness" (Genesis 15:6). This is precisely the same way the New Testament believers are saved through obedience and faith for God's calling is always a step of faith in that leads sinners to repentance.

Thus is Abram's seed divided into two for by faith does His seed represent every believer throughout all generations who are spiritually born into God's promise of redemption through Christ. Yet as Abram was the first Jew, there is also a physical fulfillment to Abram's seed. God unconditionally promised that Abram's natural descendants and progeny would come out of slavery and possess the land of Canaan, "In the same day the Lord made a covenant with Abram, saying, Unto thy seed have I given

---

[60] John Gill Commentary, ibid., Genesis 12:1, (accessed August 28, 2018).

this land, from the river of Egypt unto the great river, the river Euphrates" (Genesis 15:18).

In the first instance, this is fulfilled through Isaac before, over time, blossoming into the great nation that God did promise, "The Lord your God hath multiplied you, and, behold, ye are this day as the stars of heaven for multitude" (Deuteronomy 1:10).

As a sign of certainty and reaffirming that God's promise will be fulfilled, Abram's name is changed in Genesis 17:5 along with Sarai's in Genesis 17:15. "God swore to keep this promise because it was a necessary step in his larger Kingdom purposes. God chose the family of Abraham to be the instrument through which his original purposes for humanity would be fulfilled" [61]

Scripture confirms God's promise that Abraham's descendants did receive this promise and successfully inherit the land to establish a great nation there, "And the Lord gave unto Israel all the land which he sware to give unto their fathers; and they possessed it, and dwelt therein" (Joshua 21:43). Righteousness before God, however, does not ensue by natural descent through Abraham's physical or natural seed for not all Israelites are born of promise in obedience to God, as the Apostle Paul surely attests, "For they are not all Israel, which are of Israel," (Romans 9:6).

So the natural land promises as given to Abraham serve as a type for the spiritual promises as believers today enter the same heavenly realm, whereby, Old Testament saints entered by faith, "These all died in faith, not having received the promises, but having seen them afar off, and were persuaded of them, and embraced them, and confessed that they were strangers and pilgrims on the earth" (Hebrews 11:13). Thus is the economy of God concerning salvation is always unchanging as all covenant promises are apprehended solely by faith.

---

[61] Dr. Richard Pratt, *God of Covenant*, ibid.

TYPICAL CHURCH: -

Throughout the Old Testament, the physical seed of Abraham runs parallel to that of the spiritual seed in blessing from God because all the promises of God were born through the nation of Israel. Our Lord was physically born of the Jews, yet after our Lord's death, however, the physical seed is removed from His providence for God's promises pertain only to the church, or spiritual Israel. This represents all believers that are effectually called and regenerated through faith in His promise of redemption.

Christ is that seed of Abraham for Grace is the true covenant that God has given the creature as remedy against sin since the Fall and is the greatest passage or biblical theme that links and joins believers from the Old Testament, or the Jewish age of the church, to those in the New Testament, "So then they which be of faith are blessed with faithful Abraham" (Galatians 3:9).

Throughout the Old Testament, therefore, the church is clearly identified in the type of national Israel, "This is he, that was in the church in the wilderness with the angel which spake to him in the mount Sinai, and with our fathers: who received the lively oracles to give unto us" (Acts 7:38). The antitype and fulfillment of the true church, however, is represented as "a remnant according to the election of Grace" (Romans 11:5) for God always preserved a true people to Himself by faith throughout the Old Testament which continues through to today.

"The church, like our salvation and like the kingdom, is old and new at the same time. In its different aspects or phases, the church can be said to be past present and future. Born in the mind of God before the foundation of the world, it came into being in the garden of Eden with the provision that Christ would come forth and meet Satan on his own ground, and defeat him (Genesis. 3:15)." [62]

---

[62] William E Cox, ibid., p. 49.

In Romans 11, The Apostle Paul alludes to 1 Kings 19 after Elijah's encounter with the prophets of Baal on Mount Carmel, where, as a measure of comfort to Elijah's despondency, the Lord says, "Yet have I left me seven thousand in Israel, all the knees that have not bowed to Baal, and every mouth that hath not kissed him" (1 Kings 19:18). The Apostle now confirms that just as there always existed a remnant in Elijah's time, reserved by God, the same remnant exists today, and it is not from anything in themselves, but solely by God's divine influence and agency that illuminated them to the promise of Grace whilst also preserving them from such surrounding bondage to outward ceremonial laws.

Election according to Grace is, therefore, an unconditional promise and sovereign choice in the favor of God. This remnant, or seed, is a gratuitous election and effectual calling into which this faithful body of believers, or true Israel, forms the definitive link between the Old Testament to the New Testament. The church of the Jews, before the birth of Christ, and the church of the Christians since, are essentially one, differing only in some outward administrations, "And that he might reconcile both unto God in one body by the cross, having slain the enmity thereby" (Ephesians 2:16). God most faithfully preserved this blessed seed throughout Old Testament times to determine His typical church: -

"so the holy seed shall be the substance thereof"
(Isaiah 6:13).

IGNORANCE: -

Aside from the blessed remnant, however, much darkness pervaded Israel through the Jewish religious leaders who, in total ignorance, went about to establish their own righteousness, "For they being ignorant of God's righteousness, and going about to establish their own righteousness, have not submitted themselves unto the righteousness of God" (Romans 10:3).

Such apostate and desolate activity actually caused the name of God to be blasphemed in them instead of being honored; "the whole land is made desolate because no man layeth it to heart" (Jeremiah 12:11). "Instead of holding all their mercies and privileges in humble dependence upon God, the scribes, high priests and Pharisees looked upon righteousness as but a moral thing, only beholding the visor, or outward show of the work, and not the heart of him that doeth the work." [63]

Such exaltation also gendered bondage through dead works to the conscience of most Jewish people. They never acknowledged their sin in repentance and faith, as Jeremiah further says, "For both prophet and priest are profane; yea, in my house have I found their wickedness, saith the Lord" (Jeremiah 23:11). A total misappropriation of God's goodness to this nation resulted, along with countless transgressions, by their continual infidelity in worshipping false idols. The Lord did continually rebuke such unfaithfulness in not submitting themselves unto the righteousness of God, "Woe unto you scribes and Pharisees, hypocrites!" (Matthew 23:23).

In urging their own righteousness, the Lord's anger is also evident throughout the Old Testament in 2 ways. Firstly, the kingdom was divided into two after the ten tribes revolted from God, "And he said to Jeroboam, Take thee ten pieces: for thus saith the Lord, the God of Israel, Behold, I will rend the kingdom out of the hand of Solomon, and will give ten tribes to thee" (1 Kings 11:31).

Secondly, and despite much grief, anguish and warning from the Prophets concerning their continued gross idolatry and disobedience to God's commandments, both the northern and southern kingdoms of Israel suffered the wrath of God and went

---

[63] Martin Luther, *Commentary on Galatians,* ibid., p. 154.

into exile. The Jews began to rebuild the temple in Jerusalem after 536 B.C. once their ensuing 70-year period of captivity had finished, which took a further 20 years to complete by 516 B.C. under the directive of the two prophets Haggai and Zechariah.

Proponents of dispensationalism uphold that such prophesies concerning the building of the temple are yet to be fulfilled but the Scripture affirms that this work was completed, "And kept the feast of unleavened bread seven days with joy: for the LORD had made them joyful, and turned the heart of the king of Assyria unto them, to strengthen their hands in the work of the house of God, the God of Israel" (Ezra (6:22).

False worship, however, remained in the temple as our Lord overturned the tables of money changers within the temple, "And said unto them, It is written, My house shall be called the house of prayer; but ye have made it a den of thieves" (Matthew 21:13). The parallels between the confusion and bondage gendered by Satan in Israel's false and ceremonial worship throughout Old Testament times is striking to such counterfeit worship of today. Many western churches have been completely infiltrated from within to follow the trends of the world as opposed to taking a wholly and separate stance. True and spiritual worship of the heart is lost when unregenerate demands of the flesh predominate within large and contemporary congregations.

During Israel's captivity through their unfaithfulness to God, Daniel's Prophesy of desolation foretells of national judgment and an end to the Jewish age of the church at the hand of Titus and his Roman army, which culminates in the destruction of the temple at Jerusalem in 70 A.D. Thus is the Lord's protective hand removed from such unbelief, "Behold your house is left unto you desolate" (Daniel 9:27).

The Lord graphically portrays this judgment, "And when ye shall see Jerusalem compassed with armies, then know that the desolation thereof is nigh. And they shall fall by the edge of the sword, and shall be led away captive into all nations: and Jerusalem shall be trodden down of the Gentiles" (Luke 21:24). Thus is all temple order and ceremonial obligation perfectly fulfilled through the atoning sacrifice of Christ, who can be worshipped freely anytime, in any place upon the heart.

Self-righteousness and pride became the Jewish religious leaders great "stumblingstone and the rock of offence" (Romans 9:33) for they were blind that true and saving faith is offered freely upon the heart. Isaiah is forceful in saying that Israel would have been destroyed in their wickedness had it not been for the blessed seed, "Except the Lord of hosts had left unto us a very small remnant, we should have been as Sodom, and we should have been like unto Gomorrah" (Isaiah 1:9). "The Jews had rejected Christ because He came not to them in the way of their carnal expectations, and, therefore, refused the grace tendered by Him." [64]

In New Testament times, unfaithful and natural Israel is thus removed from His providence, "Therefore, I say unto you, the Kingdom of God shall be taken from you, and given to a nation bringing forth the fruits thereof" (Matthew 21:43). This change was determined to bring about more glory to Himself in that the fabric of faith as seen through the faithful remnant of Israel joined with Gentiles at Pentecost to receive a greater body of Gentile believers into the fold of Christ in this present Gospel age, "And it shall come to pass in the last days, saith God, I will pour out of my Spirit upon all flesh" (Acts 2:17).

There is no more localization of God's people for the accomplishment of Calvary is now globalized but as in Old Testament times through God's mercy, the remnant of Jewish Christians coming to a saving knowledge of Christ through repentance and faith still permeates today, for "God hath not cast away his people which he foreknew" (Romans 11:2). Jews, like all other Gentiles, are grafted into the vine by faith.

---

[64] A.W. Pink, ibid., p. 29.

Generic descent has nothing to do with the spiritual seed of Abraham for "God has not suspended His purpose for national Israel, He has fulfilled it and is fulfilling it in the remnant, or true Israel of the church." [65] This casting of Israel according to the flesh from God's providence is clearly confirmed by the Apostle Paul: -

"They which are the children of the flesh, these are not the children of God: but the children of the promise are counted for the seed" (Romans 9:8).

It is also not a replacement or superseding theology concerning Israel throughout the Jewish age of the church to the Gentile age of today because the true church as represented by the spiritual seed of Grace always existed, and as symbolic of the greater fulfillment to come, a number of non-Jewish or Gentile believers were saved throughout the Old Testament, like Ruth, Naaman, Nebuchadnezzar, and Rahab. Thus does God's sovereign mercy determine a unified body of believers, both visible and invisible, that make up the church down the history of time.

The visible church comprise of all believers of today, both Jew and Gentile, that make up the perpetual seed, who in true repentance, have turned from their sin and walk in faith. The invisible church represents all believers now at rest in heaven as disembodied souls awaiting our Lord's glorious return. When "the fullness of the Gentiles be come in," (Romans 11:25) ""all Israel" shall be converted and saved, and a nation shall be born at once; then will God show himself to them as their covenant God, manifest his love to them, and bestow the blessings of his Grace upon them." [66] "And ye shall be my people, and I will be your God" (Jeremiah 30:22).

[65] Keith A Mathison, *Dispensationalism, Rightly Dividing The People of God?* P&R Publishing, 1995, p. 30.
[66] John Gill Commentary, ibid., Jeremiah 31:1 , (accessed January 9, 2019).

TEMPLE SACRIFICE: -

All temple sacrifice has ceased for Christ is that perfect and everlasting sacrifice made on behalf of others, "And the veil of the temple was rent in twain from the top to the bottom" (Mark 15:38). Any sacrifice outside of God's kind provision in Christ is, therefore, an abomination and all covenant fulfillment depends upon His faithfulness and sovereign timing and ways, not creature politics. Prophesy cannot be forced into reality which is the fundamental the error of dispensationalism in concluding that all of God's promises and Prophesy throughout the Old Testament pertain only to the Jews and not the wider church.

A greater error still is the means by which Old Testament Scripture is corrupted to justify this political end as the force of God's Word is severely blunted when biblical history is considered as divided by God into seven different dispensations and defined periods or ages to which God has allotted distinctive administrative principles. "The literalism which insists on the Old Testament prophesies being referred to the Israel after the flesh, is utterly inconsistent with the universal New Testament application of the promises to the spiritual seed." [67]

The Jews do not need Christians pointing them to Jerusalem for a political and modern day Palestine, they need believer's pointing them to Christ which, in God's unchanging economy, is always by Grace! Yet God's blessing of true Israel into this Gospel age, against the perpetual hardening of unbelieving Jews and the removal of His protective hand in judgment toward them, serves as great and sovereign warning in three ways: -

Firstly, it forbids other Gentile nations to neglect so great an offer of mercy during this present Gospel age, "Behold therefore the goodness and severity of God, on them which fell severity; but

---

[67] W.J Grier, ibid., p. 50.

toward thee goodness, if thou continue in his goodness: otherwise thou shall be cut off" (Romans 11:22).

Secondly, it also serves as a great encouragement to believing Israelites, or the remnant themselves according to the election of Grace, for as concerning the Gospel, unbelieving Israelites are, "enemies for your sakes" (Romans 11:28) to try and purify their faith amidst such impenitence and false worship. They are also "beloved for the father's sakes" (Romans 11:28) for their obstinate unbelief proves the promise of Grace to their fathers Abraham, Isaac, and Jacob that a promised seed would follow by Grace.

Thirdly, and ever willing for Israelites to be saved, Paul emphasizes that the example of the Gentiles in receiving such mercy may invigorate unbelieving Jews to cleave to Christ and, like Old Testament times, again be mercifully received of His providence, "that through your mercy they also may obtain mercy" (Romans 11:31). Against such threat of condemnation, the prayer of New Testament believers is that many more Jews would repent of their sin in salvation for which the Apostle is ecstatic in praise: -

> "O the depth of the riches both of the wisdom
> and knowledge of God! How unsearchable are
> his judgments, and his ways past finding out!'
> (Romans 11:33).

UNITED BODY OF BELIEVERS: -

Despite spiritual darkness surrounding the nation of Israel from their religious leaders, along with that nation's infidelity with foreign and strange gods, the promised seed of Grace gives rise believers throughout the Jewish age of the church and continues to all Gentile lands today by faith: -

"And as many as walk according to this rule,
peace be on them, and mercy, and upon the Israel
of God" (Galatians 6:16).

Satan cannot overthrow nor prevent this spread for he is restrained from doing so as this is the true covenant by which God's faithful and sovereign mercy are linked with believers throughout Old Testament times or true Israel, to Gentile believers in New Testament times for all are united in the body of Christ: -

"seeing it is one God, which shall justify the
circumcision by faith, and uncircumcision
through faith" (Romans 3:30).

This is the true covenant of God that Satan cannot divide as Christ and His people form a single and regenerate body of believers according to the election of Grace from the Old Testament to the New. It is a sovereign link which our minds' eye of faith further confirms, for believers "look not at the things that are seen, but at the things that are not seen, for the things that are seen are temporal, but the things that are not seen are eternal" (2 Corinthians 4:18). The Spirit persuaded Old Testament saints of the same promise by faith before its fulfillment in Christ. New Testament saints are persuaded of its fulfillment, but it is a unification by faith alone: -

"for the just shall live by faith" (Romans 1:17).

"God has written and preserved the history of the Jews throughout the Old Testament to teach the church how he deals with His people spiritually." [68] "If thou wilt diligently hearken to the voice of the Lord thy God, and wilt do that which is right in

---

[68] Peter Masters, *Not Like Any Other Book*, Wakeman Trust, 2004, p. 57.

his sight, and wilt give ear to his commandments, and keep all his statutes, I will put none of these diseases upon thee, which I have brought upon the Egyptians: for I am the Lord that healeth thee" (Exodus 15:26).

God's promise of redemption as first seen in Scripture as seed in Genesis 3:15 eventually blossoms into a beautiful flower and branch of our Lord's Life, death and resurrection. New Testament believers have the blessing of seeing all of God's progressive revelation as fully revealed and made manifest in Christ, for each phase of the church, although different in outward appearance from the Jewish age to this current Gentile age through to the future glorified state of the church, all bear the same framework of redemption through Him.

The first covenant of works represents a "ministration of condemnation," because man cannot uphold such righteous obedience before God. But so much more does that which remains, namely Grace, as "the ministration of righteousness exceed in glory" (2 Corinthians 3:9). Grace is enacted through the covenant of redemption and the conditions by which are met through what Christ has fulfilled in perfect obedience in His agreement with the Father. It is the great underlying link and thread throughout Scripture in reconciliation to God for Grace not only abounds the Abrahamic covenant but is also seen right alongside the Mosaic covenant: -

THE ABRAHAMIC COVENANT: -

As with all believer's, Abraham was called out from his previous life by God, "The God of glory appeared unto our father Abraham, when he was in Mesopotamia, before he dwelt in Charran" (Acts 7:2). Similar to all believers as well, Abraham was a sinner and would have perished as such unless God's sovereign mercy did not graciously call him to repentance. There is, therefore, a dual nature to the Abrahamic covenant for Abraham was regarded by God as the head of the Jewish nation. Concerning his spiritual seed, Grace is revealed through obedience and circumcision in the heart to the promises of God, "For what saith the scripture? Abraham believed God, and it was counted unto him for righteousness" (Romans 4:3). This blessed seed perpetuates today throughout all Gentile lands in the effectual call of the Gospel unto repentance and faith.

Conversely, the natural fulfillment of Abraham's seed represents his descendants who did physically populate the nation of Israel. This natural seed bore much affliction, and perverted such virtue and privilege before God, through disobedience of the heart, 'Ye stiffnecked and uncircumcised in heart and ears, ye do always resist the Holy Ghost: as your fathers did, so do ye,' (Acts 7:51). God's providence eventually ceased to leave this physical as seed strangers to God's promises and desolate, although His ever faithful offer of mercy to the Jews to become Christian in true and saving faith still abides today.

The obstinate Jews claim to have Abraham as their father but they do not have the faith of Abraham which leaves the ancient Jewish belief that their physical and natural descent counted towards God's Kingdom as groundless for all of God's true seed are spiritually born and regenerate by Grace.

Divine promises are made, "And I will make thee exceeding fruitful, and I will make nations of thee, and kings shall come out of thee" (Genesis 17:6) but in the same way that the Davidic line is also required to "keep my covenant" (Psalm 132:11) the covenant also places the direct and conditional stipulation of circumcision upon Abraham and his descendants as a picture, or type, of obedience in that anybody who does not obey this covenant would be cut off and placed under covenant curses, "that soul shall be cut off from his people; he hath broken my covenant" (Genesis 17:14).

Abraham's carnal act with Hagar in Genesis 16 would not have caused God to return to him with explicit explanations and threats in the very next chapter. Moses' account of Genesis 17, thereby, addresses the responsibility of Abraham and future generations of Israelites following him in conforming to the moral requirements of God, as also prescribed later through the various rites and ceremonies of the Mosaic law that were designed to teach the Israelites of holiness, "Thou shalt be perfect with the Lord thy God" (Deuteronomy 18:13).

The New Testament, therefore, perfectly clarifies the interrelating relationship between the Old Testament, "But he is a Jew, which is one inwardly; and circumcision is that of the heart, in the spirit, and not in the letter; whose praise is not of men, but of God" (Romans 2:29). Genuine circumcision is always spiritual and inward, and only a reviving work of Grace upon the soul brings true glory to God. "Not the law of God in the hand, but in the heart; not an external righteousness only, but internal holiness; and who is not a mere outward court worshipper, but a worshipper of God in Spirit and in truth." [69]

Thus did Abraham sojourn by faith "in the land of promise, as in a strange country, dwelling in tabernacles with Isaac and Jacob, the heirs with him of the same promise" (Hebrews 11:9). sojourning in tents, the patriarchs waited in faithful anticipation of a heavenly Inheritance and is why in full obedience was Abraham's household circumcised "that selfsame day, as God had said unto him" (Genesis 17:23).

Yet the Apostle Paul declares that Abraham "received the sign of circumcision, a seal of the righteousness of the faith which he had yet being uncircumcised: that he might be the father of all them that believe, though they be not circumcised; that righteousness might be imputed unto them also" (Romans 4:11). As with Abraham, all believers, both Jew, and Gentile alike are sealed in the righteousness of faith made without circumcision.

Abraham's obedience is further seen before offering Isaac on the altar of sacrifice where, in response to Isaac's inquiry as to the

---

[69] John Gill Commentary, ibid., Romans 2:29 (accessed October 23, 2018).

whereabouts of the lamb for the burnt offering, Abraham said, "God will provide himself a lamb for a burnt offering" (Genesis 22:8) before offering his son Isaac was on the altar of sacrifice. Yet it was "a lamb caught in the thickets by its horns" that was sacrificed (Genesis 22:13) as a picture of our Savior's all-sufficient sacrifice at Calvary.

The promised seed does carry forward to Isaac who, as spiritual heir, is blessed by Almighty God, "And I will make thy seed to multiply as the stars of heaven...and in thy seed shall all the nations of the earth be blessed; Because that Abraham obeyed my voice, and kept my charge, my commandments, my statutes, and my laws" (Genesis 26:4-5).

Abraham stood as regenerate and justified in faithful anticipation to God's promise of redemption and is both a picture of Grace and a father of many nations because of his seed that is born by faith into such a promise. Christ is that very seed for His offering once made for sin appeases God's wrath, whereby, all believers inherit the blessing of Abraham through faith, "He saith not, And to seeds, as of many; but as of one, And to thy seed, which is Christ" (Galatians 3:16). Grace always abounded this promise, "For if the inheritance is of the law, it is no more of promise: but God gave it to Abraham by promise" (Galatians 3:18).

The covenant of Grace is never revoked but remains as sure as ever, and faithful Abraham, which represents all true believers, receive covenant blessings by faith, by which our curse of sin is forever removed through Christ's blood, "As far as the east is from the west, so far hath he removed our transgressions from us,' (Psalms 103:12).

THE MOSAIC COVENANT: -

We have already considered how Adam's transgression of God's command relating to the knowledge of good and evil in the garden of Eden at the fall did bear original sin into the world and impute death as a consequence. A promise of redemptive Grace is immediately given by God against the broken covenant of works as the remedy for sin (Genesis 3:15), yet God's holy, righteous and just character is further revealed in the Ten Commandments, which He wrote on tablets of stone as instructed to Moses on Mount Horeb. The Commandments thus contained in the Decalogue are a declaration of God's moral law and are for all people and for all time.

God institutes social order through the civil or criminal law in the Old Testament, along with the many and various sacrificial laws, rites and ordinance ascribed through the Levitical priesthood to establish temple worship, that set God's people apart as holy and peculiar to Himself. "Christianity lay in Judaism as leaves and fruit do in the seed, though certainly, it needed the divine sun to bring them forth." [70]

Moses fully declares both blessings in obedience to this covenant and curses for not, "Behold, I set before you this day a blessing and a curse, A blessing, if ye obey the commandments of the Lord your God...And a curse, if ye will not obey the commandments of the Lord your God, but turn aside out of the way...to go after other gods, which ye have not known" (Deuteronomy 11:26-28). Curses did abound the natural seed of Israel through their continual infidelity with idolatry and their self-righteous fixation with the ancient sacrificial law which could only remove ceremonial uncleanness, not uncleanness of heart. "And all the house of Israel are uncircumcised of heart" (Jeremiah 9:26).

Nobody can begin to uphold, much less finish, such duty and moral scrutiny as required by the precepts of God's law except one, namely, the Lord Jesus Christ who lived a perfect life of

---

[70] Patrick Fairbairn, *The Typology of Scripture*, Vol. 1, Evangelical Press, 1975, p. 34.

obedience to fulfil all manner of righteousness, as David declares, "Be surety for thy servant for good: let not the proud oppress me" (Psalm 119:122). His atoning sacrifice, that both purges the conscience and restores life to the soul, is immediately pre-figured after the Mosaic law is declared: -

"An altar of earth thou shalt make unto me, and shalt sacrifice thereon thy burnt offerings, and thy peace offerings, thy sheep, and thine oxen: in all places where I record my name I will come unto thee, and I will bless thee" (Exodus 20:24).

Thus does our Lord stand at the apex of history for just as believers today look back through the lens of completion by faith and are justified in His sacrifice for sin at Calvary; Old Testament believers looked forward in anticipation to the same promise of redemption for sin. It all emanates from the covenant of redemption, by which our fathers, in true repentance, did apprehend the Son of God by faith, and: -

> "did all drink the same spiritual drink: for they
> drank of that spiritual Rock that followed them:
> and that Rock was Christ" (1 Corinthians 10:4).

"Such being the idea of a sacrifice which pervades the whole Jewish Scriptures, it is obvious that the sacred writers could not teach more distinctly and intelligibly the manner in which Christ secures the pardon of sin than by saying He was made an offering for sin. With this mode of pardon, all the early readers of the Scriptures were familiar...Not one of them could recall the time when the altar, the victim, and the blood were unknown to him." [71]

A great price had to be paid to secure our release for unlike a slave who was set free in former days by a declared price of money or gold, Christ freely became a curse for us to release His people, "being made a curse for us: for it is written, Cursed is every one

---

[71] Charles Hodge, ibid., p. 7.

that hangeth on a tree" (Galatians 3:13). Also, despite our Lord's innocence before the law, His death was intensified as the curse of God was inflicted upon Him to liberate believer's from all guilt and condemnation from the law.

His precious blood settles our account in full with God which means that blood shedding in circumcision is finished for we may now use water in the ordinance and seal of baptism and wine in the Lord's supper. There is also no more ceremonial blood-shedding with Passover lambs, for the Lord's blood was shed which is all-sufficient for the remission of sin.

Not only were the promises of God first given to Israel but the Lord's sovereign purpose for the nation of Israel is also served by the administration of the sacrificial law, "which was a figure for the time then present, in which were offered both gifts and sacrifices, that could not make him that did the service perfect, as pertaining to the conscience" (Hebrews 9:2). These sacrifices, as offered daily, were imperfect, ineffectual and stood as mere shadows that pointed to a greater fulfillment by our Savior: -

"For by one offering he hath perfected them for
ever that are sanctified" (Hebrews 10:14).

Perfect obedience and observation are impossible by rites and ceremonial sacrifice as Moses confirms, "Cursed be he that confirmeth not all the words of this law to do them" (Deuteronomy 27:26). The Apostle then applies Moses words to prove that Grace is the definitive link between Old Testament to the New, otherwise does the curse always remain, "For as many as are of the works of the law are under the curse: for it is written, Cursed is every one that continueth not in all things which are written in the book of the law to do them" (Galatians 3:10).

Christian righteousness is, therefore, obtained by faith freely given upon the heart as Moses further declares, "the Lord thy God shall circumcise thine heart, and the heart of thy seed, to love the Lord thy God with all thine heart, and with all thy soul, that thou mayest live" (Deuteronomy 30:6).

Only the Lord can circumcise the heart of a believer by faith, for mercy is directed by the will of Him that showeth mercy which determines God's covenant people, "But the scripture hath concluded all under sin, that the promise by faith of Jesus Christ might be given to them that believe" (Galatians 3:22). The priesthood of Christ is always unchanging for salvation is always of Grace!

CHAPTER 7

GRACE FOR GRACE

It is such a blessed notion to consider that believers can grow in Grace, "Therefore if any man be in Christ, he is a new creature: old things are passed away; behold, all things are become new" (2 Corinthians 5:17). The act of God in our regeneration is so momentous that no single category of thought is sufficient to describe the changes it brings about in and for the soul every believer. We are born again as citizens of Jesus Christ and, thereby, translated from spiritual death to life, changed as from darkness to light. We are granted wisdom and a new nature that can overcome the tyranny of sin, and we have a new found prayer life that forms the foundation of our dependency and worship of Him. Eternally, our condemnation is forever removed for sin and we stand as citizens of heaven before the Father who now sees us through the perfect righteousness Christ.

Misery and wretchedness before God, however, is the result of sin and under the righteous government of God, and no one is cursed who does not deserve to be because of unbelief. This, in turn, highlights the restraint of Satan because he cannot prevent God's pity and mercy in relieving His redeemed from such condemnation. God's holy and righteous character as expressed through the law pronounces guilt upon all and deserving of eternal wrath, "Now we know that what things soever the law saith, it saith to them who are under the law: that every mouth may be stopped, and all the world may become guilty before God" (Romans 3:19).

God's law is always good for it because it is clothed with divine authority that utters the mandates of His will. His true and holy character is thus revealed against which His justice does stand and abide as seen in two ways: -

Firstly, the civil and moral use of the law bridles wickedness and increases transgression to show our hopeless end that we might have an entrance into Grace. Before conversion, a sinner is driven outside of himself to see the reality of his fallen nature, "Nay, I had not known sin but by the law" (Romans 7:7). It crushes man to show the absolute gravity and sinfulness of sin "For sin, taking occasion commandment, deceived me, and by it slew me...that sin by the commandment might become exceeding sinful" (Romans 7:11-13).

The law is a ministration of death from which God's divine favor and effectual call inexhaustibly abound by Grace in saving sinners from our natural and carnal state in the flesh. The deserved wrath of God abides, but for this pardon, as the creature's greatest problem mirrors that of the Jews which is disobedience of the heart, for "Whosoever committeth sin transgresseth also the law: for sin is the transgression of the law" (1 John 3:4).

Secondly, sanctifying Grace manifests in such a way after conversion that the law, which is good and holy, becomes a believer's moral compass through peace and meditation, "For I delight in the law of God after the inward man" (Romans 7:22). An almighty battle has now commenced against such peace, however, for the flesh, comprising of our old sin nature, will battle and entwine against the newness and direction of the Spirit.

The Apostle was acutely aware of the bondage gendered when works are substituted for the atonement of Christ as the ground of justification, "O foolish Galatians, who hath bewitched you, that ye should not obey the truth, before whose eyes Jesus Christ hath been evidently set forth, crucified among you?" (Genesis 3:1).

Although the Galatians were Gentile believers, it was the pull of the flesh against the Spirit, through the agency of enchanting Judaizers, who taught that adopting Jewish customs and practices of the law was necessary for salvation. This why the Apostle calls them accursed to be living as carnal against the merit and liberty they had already found in Christ.

THE LAW OF SIN: -

This reproof applies to believers today as we too can be easily bewitched and led astray and from our privilege and liberty in Christ, "seeing they crucify to themselves the Son of God afresh, and put him to an open shame" (Hebrews 6:6). No believer can afford to be passive for Satan sometimes ensnares in the flesh which can quickly lead towards moral decline. The conscience of a believer is sensitive against sin but any such foothold that Satan does gain is spiritually dangerous for which the Apostle exhorts believers to put on God's full armor of faith in order to be fully equipped for this spiritual warfare: -

> "that ye may be able to stand in the evil day,
> having done all, to stand" (Ephesians 6:13).

Whilst a believer does have unspeakable joy and everlasting assurance in Christ, this battle of the flesh and an inclination towards evil is something that will follow all the days of his life. This dilemma, that sin, like a foreign intruder, will always try to lure itself back into a believer's soul to bring you down. A believer is certainly at peace with God but is never at peace with sin.

In overcoming this, the Apostle states that the fulfillment of the law boils down to one command, "to love one another: for he that loveth another hath fulfilled the law" (Romans 13:8). We cannot possibly uphold this in our own strength for which we need the knowledge of the truth of Christ as the perfect law-keeper in obedience to secure us like a belt as the best antidote to stand against Satan's lies and deception. "Having your loins girt about with truth, and having on the breastplate of righteousness" (Ephesians 6:14). This is inward and spiritual health when the Spirit in co-operating with ordinance distills Grace upon our hearts.

The law of Christ is not an extensive list of legal codes, it is a law of love. If we love God with all our heart, soul, mind, and strength, we will do nothing to displease Him. If we love our neighbors as ourselves, we will do nothing to harm them. The law of Christ is not a requirement to earn or maintain salvation but obedience to the law of Christ is what God expects of a Christian: –

"Verily I say unto you, Whatsoever ye shall bind on earth shall be bound in heaven: and whatsoever ye shall loose on earth shall be loosed in heaven" (Matthew 18:18).

It is not restrictive or coercive, but through the law does a believer find liberty in imitating God and His holiness, and as our Savior's unconditional love did fulfill and uphold all moral commands, so does James instruct us likewise, "If ye fulfil the royal law according to the scripture, Thou shalt love thy neighbour as thyself, ye do well" (James 2:8). The territory is marked for believers in that those that do delight and obey His commands, Satan will actually "flee from you" (James 4:7).

THE SAFETY OF THE GODLY: -

Believers are given the authority and protection of Christ to stand against the wiles of the Devil in yielding themselves to bear salt and light in this darkened world which is the Lord's sovereign purpose through His people on earth to bring glory to Himself. Obedience to God's moral law as a rule of life is fundamental to living a sanctified Christian life, for which He grants much protection and discernment to abide: -

> "But the anointing which ye have received of him abideth in you, and ye need not that any man teach you: but as the same anointing teacheth you of all things, and is truth, and is no lie" (1 John 2:27).

This abiding must stem from a corporate level for the wisdom and function of the local church is to edify, teach and instruct believers against error in standing for the truth. The devil hates the biblical doctrine of separation from teaching because he is the father of lies and author of confusion. Believers must certainly have pity and concern for all who are ensnared in error as Jude warns about false Christians, pointing out that some may be savable. Save such he says, "with fear, pulling them out of the fire; hating even the garment spotted by the flesh" (Jude v: 23). "The rule of scripture is that we must reach out to non-evangelical 'Christians' as outsiders, but that we never do or say anything which would condone, flatter, dignify or recognise their false teaching." [72]

We are justified by faith alone, in Christ alone, apart from works, to grow in faith and holiness by keeping God's holy commands. We delight in doing so out of deep gratitude bestowed upon us by Christ. Nothing can add to, or take away from, justification, the other side of conversion, however, is the gradual growth in Grace, for which sanctification is a lifelong process for the believer: -

> "We beseech you brethren, that you increase more and more" (1 Thessalonians 4:10).

Whilst we do have great assurance in Christ and His victory over sin, death, and hell, Satan will be intently watching every

---

[72] Peter Masters, *Stand for the Truth*, Wakeman Trust, 2008, p. 9.

move of a believer from the point a profession of faith is made. He is not overly concerned with the general mass walking in accordance to the whims and fashions of this passing world, but it is when a believer begins to walk contrary to this that his immediate attention and guile is drawn.

It is akin to a tug of war against Satan for every believer has a residue of sin, as our old sin nature still clings to a believer against his will. Sanctification is a hard fought process of the heart to overcome our habitual and perpetual master sins that were willingly followed, practiced or worshipped for years before conversion. To uphold the holy law of God, believers have a double assurance that Grace shall prevail through the imputed righteousness of Christ along with the blessings of the Holy Spirit, "God is faithful who will not suffer you to be tempted above what you are able; but will with the temptation also make a way to escape, that ye may be able to bear it" (1 Corinthians 10:13). We must stand in dependence on Him who is the perfect moral example.

The New Testament, thereby, provides many statements of truth and commands that give rise to certain imperative instructions that we, as God's people, must uphold in our walk of faith. The following 6 examples are elementary yet imperative commands towards sanctification and living in a Godly manner: -

1. Holiness is essential to saving faith, "Be ye holy for I am holy" (1 Peter 1:16). Obedience in faith is pivotal in the Christian life to mirror His holy and undefiled nature, "Blessed are they which do hunger and thirst after righteousness: for they shall be filled" (Matthew 5:6). Spiritual growth is fostered by spending time in God's Word along with a dependence on God that cultivates true fellowship and sweet and Spirit-filled communion.

2. Believers are to be guided and led by the Spirit in prayer, "Praying always with all prayer and supplication in the

Spirit" (Ephesians 6:18). Prayer must always resonate from the heart in adoration to Christ, along with a confession of sin and thanksgiving for our union with Christ. Supplication not only pleads for the spiritual needs of others but also asks the gracious Spirit to lead and direct us in accordance with His will.

3. Gratefulness shows our praise and dependence upon His mercy to sustain us, whilst also stirring ourselves in the knowledge and truth of God's love in fulfilling our atonement, "Keep yourselves in the love of God, looking for the mercy of our Lord Jesus Christ unto eternal life" (Jude verse: 21).

4. Compassion is imperative in the lives of others around us, our neighbors and family for great witness and testimony are shown by our gracious, kind actions, and demeanor. Faith is proven by such compassion and understanding as to the spiritual plight of others around, "And of some have compassion, making a difference" (Jude verse: 22).

5. "Not forsaking the assembling of ourselves together, as the manner of some is; but exhorting one another: and so much the more, as ye see the day approaching" (Hebrews 10:25). Through the strong bond of fellowship, believers are able to glean blessed guidance, refinement, and edification from each other.

6. Finally, our feet must be on the go and ready to take action in winning souls for the Kingdom, "And your feet shod with the preparation of the gospel of peace" (Ephesians 6:15). Yet when ministering and reaching out to others, we are to be guarded against becoming too overly involved and pulled down by the inclination to sin, the general lifestyle, or heresy of the unsaved. In loving and getting alongside sinners for Christ sake, great humility and discernment need to be shown in drawing a clear line to guard ourselves against such unbelief which, as our Lord

instructs, already condemns them "Even the very dust of your city, which cleaveth on us, we do wipe off against you" (Luke 10:11).

DEPENDENCE: -

Both Moses and Daniel shine two amazing examples of dependence that burn as bright and faithful lights amidst the Devil's lair of darkness and deceit here on earth. Nobody is perfect in the flesh but the degree of dependence that these saints displayed in being God's chosen leaders to overcome the trials and the sin of others around, is why they are such examples of faith by fully walking in the measure of sanctifying Grace bestowed upon them. They proved the Lord time and time again in faithfulness and devotion to Him, by which the Lord mightily blessed them with more Grace upon the heart to continue in their labors, "And of his fullness have all we received, and grace for grace" (John 1:16).

Dependence is thus pivotal in maintaining a blessed and obedient walk for Satan will try everything to wear a believer down through the constant trials and busyness of everyday life. Depending upon God's strength and power to counter Satan is far more effective than standing upon our own feeble means, "Stand fast therefore in the liberty wherewith Christ has made us free, and be not entangled again with yoke of bondage" (Galatians 5:1). "As our strength abates, so the strength of Christ grows in us. When we are quite emptied of our own strength, then are we full of Christ's strength." [73]

MOSES: -

"The Lord thy God will raise up unto thee a
Prophet from the midst of thee, of thy brethren,

---
[73] William Tyndale, Ibid., p. 90.

like unto me; unto him ye shall hearken" (Deuteronomy 18:15).

Moses is a type of Christ, who was a great mediator between God and His chosen people, the Israelites, "And be ready against the third day: for the third day the Lord will come down in the sight of all the people upon mount Sinai" (Exodus 19:11). Once the moral law was given, along with many and various ancient rites and sacrifice, Moses immediately speaks of Grace against such temple order and ceremonies which was Israel's great error in seeking righteousness through such ceremony and believing that God's privilege was exclusively for them through natural descent, "These are the words of the covenant, which the Lord commanded Moses to make with the children of Israel in the land of Moab, beside the covenant which he made with them in Horeb" (Deuteronomy 29:1).

Covenant blessings are apprehended by faith and new birth, not works, as Moses attests, "It is not in heaven, that thou shouldest say, Who shall go up for us to heaven, and bring it unto us, that we may hear it, and do it? Neither is it beyond the sea, that thou shouldest say, Who shall go over the sea for us, and bring it unto us, that we may hear it, and do it?" (Deuteronomy 30:12-13). The Apostle Paul confirms Moses words that true and saving faith is always obedience of the heart, "But what saith it? The word is nigh thee, even in thy mouth, and in thy heart: that is, the word of faith, which we preach" (Romans 10:8).

Moses led the children of Israel through the waters of the Red Sea, and out of bondage and captivity towards the promised land. The typical church is seen through the people of Israel as a wholly distinct and set apart, with means and ordinances for producing and preserving acquaintance with God, obedience to His will, and hope in His promises. Christ now conducts believers through the waters of baptism into fellowship with Him, that they may be taught in duty and trained for immortality. Moses restores the altars of God, delivers laws, institutes sacrifices; and Christ erects a visible church, with ordinances and sacraments, that Gentiles may be confirmed in truth.

Spurgeon says that "Moses was a prophet indeed who yielded his life in complete service to God's People. He lived to be 120 years old by which his life can be divided into three periods of 40 years. The first 40 he spent as the son of Pharaoh's daughter in the courts of Egypt. The second 40 in the wilderness as a shepherd at the foot of Horeb. Finally, he served as leader of the Lord's People in leading them out of Egypt to the edge of the Promised land and it is this last 40 years that was crowded with events and much trial. A great man, indeed, was Moses in what he saw, and did, and said, and suffered. His life was spent in unmeasured toil; from the day when he first went into Pharaoh, till he climbed the steeps of Nebo, he must have been, night and day, incessantly engaged, and yet he finished his life-work with a song!" [74]

It is undeniable that Moses' dependence upon God through prayer is what enabled him to counter such adversity, unbelief and unmeasured toil in leading the Israelites to the foot of the promised land, "Give ear, O ye heavens, and I will speak; and hear, O earth, the words of my mouth" (Deuteronomy 32:1).

DANIEL: -

In like manner, did Daniel display similar dependence over a long period of time where the Lord placed him in a position of high authority within the administration of different Gentile rulers like Nebuchadnezzar king of Babylon and Darius the Mede. Within the captivity of a foreign land that worshipped false idols he remained faithful and was found faultless, so much so that his enemies sought his life by bringing in a decree to prevent his true

---

[74] Charles Spurgeon, *Israel's God and God's Israel*, From The Metropolitan Tabernacle Pulpit, Sermon no 803, 29/03/1868.

worship, "Now, O king, establish the decree, and sign the writing, that it be not changed, according to the law of the Medes and Persians, which altereth not" (Daniel 6:8).

As a measure of his faithfulness, Daniel prays throughout this trial, "Now when Daniel knew that the writing was signed, he went into his house; and his windows being open in his chamber toward Jerusalem, he kneeled upon his knees three times a day, and prayed, and gave thanks before his God, as he did aforetime" (Daniel 6:10). Thus did the Lord preserve his life through the lion's den, "My God hath sent his angel, and hath shut the lions' mouths, that they have not hurt me" (Daniel 6:22). The record of his later Prophetical writings have been a source of intrigue and debate for many Bible scholars but his most wonderful prayer of confession and dependence is also recorded in the midst: -

> "And I prayed unto the Lord my God, and made my confession, and said, O Lord, the great and dreadful God, keeping the covenant and mercy to them that love him, and to them that keep his commandments;"

> "We have sinned, and have committed iniquity, and have done wickedly, and have rebelled, even by departing from thy precepts and from thy judgments:"

> "Neither have we hearkened unto thy servants the prophets, which spake in thy name to our kings, our princes, and our fathers, and to all the people of the land."

> "O Lord, righteousness belongeth unto thee, but unto us confusion of faces, as at this day; to the men of Judah, and to the inhabitants of Jerusalem, and unto all Israel, that are near, and that are far off, through all the countries whither thou hast

driven them, because of their trespass that they
have trespassed against thee" (Daniel 9:4-7).

Daniel was obedient to God throughout captivity through
such prayer, for not only is real prayer an act of worship, but to
call upon His holy name and incline our will to His is to own
His goodness and His power. In seeking such spiritual blessing
and sustenance is to also acknowledge our absolute dependence
upon Him as the fundamental means of growing in Grace, as the
Apostle Paul surely attests: -

> "But by the grace of God I am what I am: and his
> grace which was bestowed upon me was not in
> vain; but I laboured more abundantly than they
> all: yet not I, but the grace of God which was with
> me" (1 Corinthians 15:10).

Countless missionaries and their families have emulated
similar obedience through prayer in their calling from the Lord
to spread His Word. Similarly, may every act of service to which
we are called be prayerfully fulfilled for He will surely guide.

Satan is a very able and cunning advocate who will try anything
to gain a foothold in our lives to, firstly, prevent us from coming
to a saving knowledge of Christ, and, secondly, after conversion,
to draw moral lapse from a believer to once again ignite our old
nature and passion of the flesh and leave our first love. We have
an abundant measure of "Grace for Grace" through the blessed
agency and communion of the Spirit to live holy and sanctified
for Him.

Yet Satan without and worldliness within the church will only
be hedged about if we stand in prayerful dependence upon Him
and prove obedience to His eternal call which is by Grace alone,
through Faith alone, in Christ alone!

BIBLIOGRAPHY

Berkhof, Louis, *A Summary of Christian Doctrine,* The Banner of Truth Trust, 1960

Calvin, John, *Commentary on Genesis,* Banner of Truth, 1965, Volume 1, p.223

Compston, Robin, God or Mammon? *The Snare of the Prosperity Gospel,* Wakeman Trust London, 2018

Cox, William E, *Amillennialism Today,* Presbyterian and Reformed Publishing Co., 1966

Creation Ministries Extra, *Whence the craziness enveloping the once-Christian west,* June 2018.

Encyclopedia Britannica (Written by the Editors of), *Biblical Translation,* https://www.britannica.com/topic/biblical-translation

Fairbairn, Patrick, *The Typology of Scripture,* Vol. 1, Evangelical Press, (Reproduced from the edition issued in New York, in 1900) First printing, June 1975

Fairbairn, Patrick, *The Visions of Ezekiel,* Wakeman Great Reprints, First published 1851

Gill, John, *Exposition of the Bible Commentary,*
https://www.biblestudytools.com/commentaries/gills-exposition-of-the-bible/

Grier, W.J, *The Momentous Event,* Banner of Truth Trust, First Published 1948 (Reprinted 2013)

Hodge, Charles, Justification, *The Law And The Righteousness of Christ*, https://www.chapellibrary.org, 1998

Lucarni, Dan, *Why I left the Contemporary Christian Music Movement*, Evangelical Press, 2002

Luther, Martin, *Commentary on Galatians*, Kregel Classics, 1979

Luther, Martin, *Commentary on Romans*, Kregel Classics, 1954

Masters, Peter, *Not Like Any Other Book*, Wakeman Trust, 2004

Masters, Peter, *Physicians of Souls*, Wakeman Trust, 2002

Masters, Peter, *Stand for the Truth*, Wakeman Trust, 2009

Mathison, Keith A, *Dispensationalism, Rightly Dividing The People of God?* P&R Publishing, 1995

Matthew McMahan, *Covenant Theology Series*, Still Water Revival Books, https://www.sermonaudio.com/sermons.asp?keyword=covenant+theology+series, Parts 1-15 02/28/1999-02/28/2006

Owen, John, (The Works of), Volume. 5, *A Display of Arminianism*, First published, 1645. http://www.puritanlibrary.com/#John%20Owen (Printed Edition, London, 1826)

Pink, A.W, *Interpretation of the Scriptures*, Baker Book House Company, 1972

Pink, A.W, *The Doctrine of Human Depravity*, https://www.chapellibrary.org, 1998

Pink, A.W, *The Sovereignty of God*, Banner of Truth Trust, Reprinted 1998

Pratt, Richard, Dr., *God of the Covenant*, Reformed Perspectives Magazine, Volume 10, Number 5, January 27 to February 2, 2008

Roberts, Maurice, *The Thought Of God*, Banner of Truth Trust, 1993

Sinclair, Ferguson B, *John Owen on the Holy Spirit, part 1 of 2*, https://www.sermonaudio.com/sermoninfo.asp?SID=112207111302, 22/11/2007

Spurgeon, C.H, *Christ the Conqueror of Satan*, From The Metropolitan Tabernacle Pulpit, Sermon no. 1326, 26/11/1876.

Spurgeon, Charles H, *Israel's God and God's Israel*, From The Metropolitan Tabernacle Pulpit, Sermon no. 803, 29/03/1868.

Tyndale, William, *Selected Works*, Focus Christian Ministries Trust, 1986

Watson, Thomas, *Body of Divinity*, Christian Classics Ethereal Library, Grand Rapids, MI, First published 1686

Williams, E.S, *The New Calvinists, Changing the Gospel*, Wakeman Trust & Belmont House, 2014

What is open theism? https://www.gotquestions.org/open-theism.html

Williams, E.S, *Holistic Mission Weighed in the Balances*, Belmont House Publishing, 2016

ABOUT THE AUTHOR

Since becaming a Christian in 2004, Lincoln has served in various ministries including both children's work and evangelical outreach.

He has a young family with 2 children and is passionate about the doctrines of Grace that promote God's glory. He has seen firsthand doctrinal error taught in several fundamental churches, and having also visited several larger contemporary churches, he has observed just how far worldliness and further doctrinal compromise has permeated the church today which has prompted him to write this book.

The subject of prayerful dependency upon God to place a hedge about Satan should concern all true professing Christians in bearing true Gospel light. May the Lord guide all His people in standing obediently to His will.

Printed in the United States
By Bookmasters